CRAZY COURAGE

A Young Widow's Survival Guide

SAMANTHA LIGHT-GALLAGHER

EDITED BY: JJ FREYERMUTH

authorHOUSE®

AuthorHouse™
1663 Liberty Drive
Bloomington, IN 47403
www.authorhouse.com
Phone: 1-800-839-8640

Published by AuthorHouse   04/03/2012

ISBN: 978-1-4685-7606-1 (sc)
ISBN: 978-1-4685-7608-5 (hc)
ISBN: 978-1-4685-7607-8 (e)

Library of Congress Control Number: 2012906208

Cover photo by Benjie Sanders – Arizona Daily Star

CONTENTS

For

Mike, my late husband
My children
And to all of the widows in the world
that believe in life after their loss

ACKNOWLEDGEMENTS

I would like to thank all the people that helped me during my "first year". This book would not have been possible without…

My children, who teach me something every day and their unconditional love.

My Mom, who has always supported me.

My Dad, who taught me the value of honesty.

My sisters, who give me the perspective I need and the strength you have showed me.

My in-laws, who welcomed me in their family and will always have a place for me.

My family that shows me love.

My friends that are always there to lean on.

The organizations that have supported my family through our unfamiliar life.

JJ, without your guidance and enthusiasm it would not have been possible to complete this book.

Other widows that have showed me their courage.

Our wedding picture. We were married in Las Vegas.

INTRODUCTION

September 2, 2010, was an ordinary day. I was working from home and remember calling Mike around 9:30 am. I was really frustrated that he didn't answer his phone when I called. I even thought about the lecture I was going to give him when he got home. What I didn't know was that he had just been struck by a drunk driver in his service vehicle. He had only been in his vehicle about four minutes after leaving the Border Patrol station near the U.S. border with Mexico.

It was around 11 am when I got the knock on my door. I remember running to the door wondering who it could be. When I opened it, the US Border Patrol was standing on my front door step. It takes the breath out of me just thinking about it. I wanted to shut the door hoping they would disappear. Instead I stood there; not knowing that what would happen next would change my life.

I looked at this man in his green uniform and noticed he was a higher ranking agent. He had sweat on his forehead and his dark eyes were difficult to read. He began to speak and I focused in on his lips. The words came out slowly. It reminds me of watching the movie Sandlot with my sons. There is a scene when the camera zooms in on a police officer's mouth as he says, "-F O R E V E R-" and everything goes into slow motion. Except the words coming out of this man's mouth now were, your husband has been in an accident. After hearing those words I looked up to find Mike's friends, agents as well, standing behind this man. I looked into their eyes and saw with disbelief the news that I didn't want to hear. Still I held onto hope that they were only going to say he was in the hospital.

The agent then asked to come in. I backed away from the door and motioned to them. I could not speak at this moment. It was as if someone was strangling me, squeezing my throat harder with every breath. My heart was racing as they entered. Around the corner came a man I did not see originally. He had a black shirt on with a notebook in his hand. I remember noticing his young face seemed very nervous. I stood in the

1

foyer as they all entered my house. The man in the black shirt looked around at the empty room and said he thought it would be better if we went in and sat down.

They followed me as I walked into the family room. I took a seat on the couch and the higher ranking agent sat next to me facing me. I watched the other man clearing toys from the floor to sit in front of me on the other side of the coffee table. I remember thinking to myself that I wished I would have cleaned up the boys mess from the night before. Our friends had taken places around me on the couch. When I looked up the higher ranking man sat up straight and looked into my eyes. The words he began to say came out like knives piercing my heart.

"I am sorry ma'am, but your husband died."

I heard myself sobbing uncontrollably, but only for a brief moment. It was a cry of hysteria, of helplessness. I remember hearing the sobs and it didn't sound like me. It was like I was hearing someone else. It brought back a memory from when I was a young teenage child. I was sitting in the hospital room with my little sister on my lap, as my grandfather was dying. My grandmother was by his side as his body went lifeless and I heard the same cry come from her. It only lasted for a brief moment, but the cry didn't sound like my grandmother. She was a widow at that moment just as I am in this moment.

Memories started whipping through my mind. It was as if I was watching the very end of an old film on a projector, when the reel is at the end and is whipping around in a circle in front of the light. What I wanted to do was wrap my arms around him to protect him. Isn't that what we are supposed to do as husband and wife? Our vows said to comfort in sickness and health. There was an aching inside to give him a hug no matter what he looked like. I say this because they kept saying to me that they did not think it was a good idea for me to see him.

I then began to remember every detail of the last time I saw him and would ever see him again alive. He wanted me to grab Egees after Quincy's football practice. I ordered his classic original grinder, a meatball sub for myself and a ham and cheese for Quincy. Rhyan was strictly a chicken nugget kid at this point, so he did not require anything from Egees. I topped us off with some ranch and chili cheese fries. Quincy and I demolished all of the ranch fries before we got home. Mike would later tease me about demolishing them and only leaving the chili cheese fries.

When I walked in the door, Rhyan was sitting on the kitchen island with his dad in front of him. I am not sure of the conversation they had but they were talking about something. I heard the belly laugh of our two year old and the look of fatherhood glowing all over Mike's face. How he was proud to teach his children new tricks. Once he was really proud of the fact that his boys would stand with pants to their knees on the back patio peeing in the grass. Often times their dad would join them. After we all dug into our food, it was time for the boys to go to sleep. While I was settling the boys into bed, Mike showered and got ready for work. I went downstairs and made our usual pot of coffee. I heard him telling the kids goodnight before he came downstairs to join me.

We went outside and sat on the patio, drinking our cups of coffee and smoking a cigarette. This was the time of day I believe we both enjoyed. We talked about our life, our plans and what we had going on in the weeks to come. This is where Mike and I continued to develop our own relationship. We had those conversations that built what we knew as our marriage and our life together. I remember him being relieved that he had met his two year probation and we were planning a three week trip to go to see both of our families. This was a new beginning for us. We were finally moving to a new stage . . . family vacations.

Before Mike left that night for work I was sitting at the computer finishing some homework. I remember how handsome he looked in his green uniform. He was off to work the night shift and I remember thinking that only a little bit longer and he moves to day shift. He knelt down and kissed me. Every time he kissed me it was so natural and I really appreciated that feeling. He stood up and turned away to walk down the hallway towards the garage. I listened to the deep clomp of his work boots hitting the tile floor. I heard him open the squeaky garage door. Then I yelled I love you and he yelled it back. I said be safe and he said he would. Then the door closed behind him and he left for another long night of work. This was the last time I saw him or heard his voice when he was alive.

Since the day my husband was killed, I have been through several stages of grief or emotional stress, or whatever anybody wants to call it. There are times when things seem so normal, but there is always something missing. All the dreams you planned together are left to do. Only now you do them on your own.

I met my husband in 2005, when I was a single mom to my son Quincy. We met while he was stationed in Fort Lewis, Washington and I lived with my sister. I was very hesitant to start a relationship with someone. My sister introduced us and we began our fairytale together. We had a son, Rhyan, in 2007. Over the years we developed a deep bond and knew each other well. I believe marriage is the most intimate bond you can have with someone. We did have our fair share of arguments or what we referred to in front of the kids as debates. Yet at the end of every day, we shared the love with each other and our children.

We spent five and a half years together and in the whole scheme of life it seems so small. However, it does not change the grief you feel inside. Grieving is a hard word to swallow. You can read about grieving. Google it and the one constant is that there are seven stages. In most of the material I read it says that people will go through each stage. I disagree. We are human; therefore each person is their own individual. I will also say that you may experience different stages of grief at the same time. I believe I have had a small dose of each stage. Each one being as difficult as the one previous and the ones that followed.

In all of the books that I have read to try to ease my pain or just make me feel a little normal, I never really felt my feelings were validated. There was one that I enjoyed and I believe it did a great job of providing stories of other young widows that I was able to relate to very well. You would think that if you meet someone that has shared the same loss you would experience it the same, but the fact is you don't. There were many days that I felt like I was on a deserted island all alone with no one around that could understand me. I only hoped that I wouldn't go crazy and paint a face on a volleyball like Tom Hanks did constantly searching for my own Wilson. There is one thing that I am fortunate to have and that is the support of my family and friends. Being able to confide in them has been very beneficial. If there is one thing that drove me crazy is that people assume there is a timeframe for things and there isn't. My closest friends and family have understood this. I think I may owe a few of them some big money for the countless hours of "therapy" they provided.

What I want to do now is provide something to those of you that are searching for some validation and to help you find your crazy courage. The following chapters are lessons and events in the last year with my personal stories pulled from my journal that might resonate with you. I will be honest and tell you all of these lessons hurt. They were some of the most painful lessons I have learned in my short life.

This book is about believing in life after your love was taken away. There were times when I would feel something inside of me saying, *I do not believe you are strong enough*. But I was strong. I just had to believe in love . . . for life and for myself.

Chapter One

CRAZY COURAGE

Face What Scares You—The Key to Crazy Courage

Defining crazy courage

Crazy courage is doing what is right for you, doing what you have to when you are in an emotional state that can become self-defeating, when you have lost the passion for life itself. Courage is when you stand up and brush the dirt off and face all the difficulty, uncertainty, and pain by overcoming the fear that has overtaken your rational mind. When you add the crazy to the courage you are adding an intense enthusiasm that will show others that you have a mission to complete, even if that mission is to get out of bed. It is when you ignore the voice that is telling you, you are not able to do it. It is not letting those fears and the pain control you anymore. It will give you the strength to surpass all of the weaknesses you may be feeling right now. The state of vulnerability you may feel is scary, but if you can learn how to eliminate that and replace it with courage you may have control again. Crazy courage is what it takes to become yourself again. It allows change to happen. Crazy courage allows you to tell yourself the truth. We may lie to ourselves so often that we begin to believe those lies. We cannot close our eyes in hopes that this will all go away. We need to listen to that crazy courage voice inside of us, the one that is telling us we can do it and ignore the voice that may be telling us we can't. We can take some deep breaths, count to ten, close our eyes and listen to what our body and mind are saying. The crazy courage inside of us may be soft whispers that are hard for us to hear, but sit long enough and you will hear them. When you hear and feel the crazy courage, pull it out and bring it to the surface. Wear it like a mask if you need to so you can get passed the first 30 seconds. You may get to a point when you no longer have to listen to the whispers and it is on the surface for you to face what scares you. If you find it difficult, you can use the crazy courage slowly. Try it out on the smaller things at first. Work your way towards bigger accomplishments. It will continue to be rewarding and continue to build within and overtake the fear. It will feel good. At times you may feel like you lost it, if you do, start over from the beginning. It is still there, just listen for your crazy courage to whisper.

I say give it 30 seconds of crazy courage and you will be surprised by what you are able to accomplish. It takes a lot of crazy courage to face those things you don't want to do, but you have to do them anyway. You're nervous, your hands are shaking, and you are ready to throw up in the nearest trash can. Crazy courage can help all of that.

This level of courage is obtainable by anyone and will be used by every widow. It's the courage you use to get out of bed and face the world again. It's the strength that you find inside yourself to do what is necessary to survive. It is usually the first 30 seconds of any situation that takes the most courage.

Think about the speeches you had to do in middle school. You felt awkward already because of puberty. The cutest boy or girl in your class sat watching you, waiting for you to speak. You felt that if you were to get in front of the class and speak it might just be the end of the world. Do you remember that feeling that in the pit of your stomach and the shaky hands you had before you started? After the first 30 seconds you usually got through those feelings and your body returned to normal and you were able to get through the rest of that moment alive.

This is what I mean by crazy courage. You need to obtain it any way possible. In certain instances I told myself that my husband, Mike would have wanted me to do this. Sometimes, I would recite in my head—'you can do it'! Sometimes I just had it. I was not sure where it came from. There are times when I needed to use it to answer my door after I heard the doorbell ring.

I believe you need to face what scares you. If you don't, you aren't going to grow as a person. You will continue to be scared and all the confidence you once had will slip away. I am not saying jump in and do everything that has scared you throughout your life. I am just saying face some of those fears right now. You have a lot to face with the loss of your spouse. Mostly you are scared, because you have lost what you once knew as your life. It left when your spouse died. It's not coming back and yes it

sucks! Acceptance and validation are crucial to crazy courage. Accepting it will take quite some time and it will not happen overnight, but when you are able to do that you will grow stronger and less afraid. I refused to accept it for a while. I did not want to admit to myself that Mike was not coming back. Yet once I allowed myself to deal with that fact, the more my courage grew. Remember that your feelings and experiences are valid. You must validate the sadness of it and face the reality. What will this do for you? It will give you back a little bit of the control that you lost in your life.

I wanted to gain some of that control back when I went to the crash site where my husband had died. A dear friend and border patrol agent, drove me the almost one and a half hours down to the scene. This was a month and a half after the crash. I didn't know what to expect and as we came near the site my body was shaking on the inside. It was as if I was on the school bus again for my first day of school completely unaware of what I was going to experience, only worse.

We drove past the site first and then circled around. He parked and we got out of the vehicle. I walked up the side of the road looking over every detail. I saw the marks in the road the pieces of debris. Were these things from the crash? I looked ahead and saw the American flag hanging from a lonely pole. This was truly a desolate place to have died. As I drew near the place where his body had laid and where he gasped for his last few breaths of air, I told myself this was not a place for anyone to have died, especially my husband. The many unanswered questions ran through my head. I tried to imagine the crash and to feel what he must have felt. Was he in any pain and why wasn't I able to be there to comfort him? His friends were by his side, but I was not. I will admit that made me jealous. For the past several years it was me who he came to for comfort and I to him. Now in his last moments it was not me—it was someone else. If I could have been the one to hold his hand and place my hand softly on his forehead rubbing my hands through his hair. I feel like I would have been able to comfort him. I knelt down in the area where I believed his body had been and scooped up some of the dirt. I placed it in a bottle and I keep that bottle tucked away behind his flag in my home now.

Facing this place scared me and it still does. It brings emotions that are hard to control, but each time I go there, it becomes easier for me. I needed to see the place where Mike had taken his last few breaths, the place where he last saw the world.

There are so many things that scare you once you feel you have lost control of your life. Out of all the things I had to do, the scariest thing by far was to face my children.

Use Your Crazy Courage

1. Take three deep breaths. Count to five with each breath in and when exhaling.
2. Tell yourself you can do it repeatedly. When alone, say it out loud and increase your volume with every phrase.
3. Remember crazy courage will help you heal in the scariest moments you will be facing.
4. Don't think too much about what you are about to do the few moments before you do the task.
5. Push yourself to find the answers to the questions that linger; it will help you heal.
6. Do not discount your desire to do the things that may be uncomfortable for others and yourself, give yourself permission to use your crazy courage.

It's okay to ask for help

HELP is written all over your face when you see people. It is audible in your voice when you talk to them as well. I can say do not be too self-conscious or too proud. I was for a long time. I was a person built to help others and felt no matter what happened I would get through this. However my friends and family were there to support me and help me anyway they could (for the most part!). Please don't feel as if you have to take on everything by yourself. There were several times that I did this and after I did, I was angry that no one asked to help. Except they did and I blew them off. You are not the only one that needs to carry the burden, lean on people. The thought brings to mind the song Lean on Me by Bill Withers and those words in the song are true.

There is an instance that I am grateful to have asked for help. I am not sure I would have been able to do it alone and when I think back I know I would not have. During the funeral planning, Mike's family and my family were there to support the decisions that were made.

There was a day that I was looking forward to, yet I dreaded at the same time. It was the day when we would go to the funeral home to determine if there would be an open casket. I am sure you might be wondering why I would look forward to something like this. It was merely to be able to see Mike one more time; to touch him. There was even a part of me that hoped it might be a mistake. I thought there might be a chance that I would walk into the room and say this is not Mike you have the wrong person. I had planned to go alone, but others had convinced me otherwise. Megan, my sister, Mike, my father-in-law and Julie, my sister-in-law came with me that day.

I can remember leaving the house filled with so much anxiety that it followed the four of us like a rain cloud. I knew that I would be facing reality yet again. Seeing Mike in the casket would validate the words I heard a few days earlier . . . your husband is dead.

We arrived at the funeral home. The door opened and a cold breeze escaped blowing on to my body. It was a hot summer day and the cool air from the building dried a little of the sweat from my face. The funeral home seemed so dark inside. I turned towards the funeral director. He motioned to the room Mike was in. I was about to walk straight in but hesitated for a moment. This was it, I would now have validation. His lifeless body would be in that room. I was not sure if he would be right by the door or further away. I remember being thankful I chose not to wear my glasses or contacts because I didn't want to recognize him until I came upon him. I took a deep breath and walked through the large doorway.

As I entered the room I noticed the pews and then the casket at the other end of the room. I saw the two honor guards that were standing on either side of the casket. They were almost like statues and moved away in unison as we walked down the pathway towards them. My sister followed close behind me with Mike's dad and Julie not far behind her. As I got closer to the casket I suddenly hit an invisible wall that brought tears and heartache. I could finally see him dressed in his green dress uniform. I forced myself to break through the wall and tears ran down my cheeks like a monsoon rain. I took the last remaining steps and came upon him. I reached out and grabbed his hand. It was stiff, cold and dead. Just like the rest of his body. At first it didn't really look like Mike, but I knew that deep down inside it was. I bent down and gave him a kiss on his forehead.

My tears dripping on to his face and I wiped them away hoping I would not ruin the make-up that covered his face. I wanted him to feel alive, it made my stomach queasy to see him lying there, not breathing, there was no heartbeat, no life, it had left his body. I reached for his hair and it felt normal to me. I rubbed my fingers through it over and over. Rubbing his hair was one thing that always comforted him. During this time my sister, Megan, stood next to me touching my shoulder for comfort. This is what I needed at that moment to survive.

But I needed more confirmation that this was truly Mike. So I moved to the top of his head and stood there peering down at him. At that moment I saw Mike just as I did a few nights before sleeping. I saw his long eyelashes that swept across his closed eyes, his jawbone and the lips that have kissed me so many times. Then I knew the reason I did not recognize him before. It was the right side of his face. All of the damage was done to that side of his face and to his nose. His nose was crooked and that was not the nose I had seen for so many years before this moment. The left side of his face was left undamaged from the crash and I remember thinking how handsome he still was even those he was lying in a casket.

Without those people to lean on that day, I am sure I could not have done it. I needed to do this to validate everything I had heard. So . . . "lean on me, when you are not strong, and I'll be your friend, I'll help you carry on".

This is a song that you should sing to yourself when you are too proud to ask for help. The people around you truly want to do something for you. It doesn't only help you, but it also helps them heal. People came over to help with yard work and my children. Something I found to be valuable were those people that drove me around. There was a day not too long after the funeral that I thought I could drive to do an errand. Well I found out that I was not capable of doing this. I was driving through town when I was pulled over by the local police. They asked me a series of questions, basically assuming I was drunk. I even got really close to the officer's face to make sure he could smell my breath and realize there was no alcohol on it. When they asked me for the registration and insurance, I pulled it from the glove box. The officer read the name and it was registered to my husband. He asked who that was and I began to cry. I told him and said that he was killed. The officer that had been standing on the passenger side this whole time, said "oh". He immediately connected the dots and realized my husband was the Border Patrol agent that was recently killed.

I wondered if he had directed traffic just days earlier for the funeral precession. He explained to the other officer that they were done here and asked me if they could give me a ride home. This was another instance that was a big eye opener for me. I realized that I could not do it all and I needed to stop being so proud.

People in your life know you need help and want to be supportive. So let them help you and lean on them. Trust me when I say there will be a time when they need to lean on you or maybe there was a time when they needed it already.

Memories of Mike also helped me. Family and friends shared their memories with me about conversations or events in their lives they shared with him. It helped me remember and learn even more about my spouse.

Use Your Crazy Courage

1. Lean on your friends and family for the support you need.
2. Do not be too proud to ask for help.
3. When your friends or family help you, you are helping them heal as well.
4. You deserve to have help.
5. Ask the widows you meet for help and guidance.

It's okay to have a bad day, bad week, even a bad month

There will be days that you don't feel like getting out of bed, or taking a shower. These days are going to happen, just let them happen. Don't be too hard on yourself. It is hard for me to let myself have these days, but we need them.

One of my favorite movies is *P.S. I Love You*. It is actually a very sad movie. It is about a woman who loses her husband to cancer. Before he died he wrote letters to her and had them sent to her for the first year after he died. He even planned a trip for her to take with her friends. A few days after Mike died I decided to watch this movie. I sat in my bed with my sister and cousin crying while I ate a whole pecan pie.

The first month was really horrible. I was in shock most of the time and cannot remember everything that happened during it. Even month two and three are a bit foggy to me. There were so many times that I just wanted to be alone. I would go a straight week without taking a shower. And so many more times that I wanted to run away from it all and hope that when I would return Mike would be there.

When you are at such an emotional low, you feel so helpless. It's almost as if you lose function of part of your brain. You feel like you are only able to breathe and use your reactionary functions. You are no longer worried if you make the bed, fold the clothes or even wear clean ones. You are going through the motions of life, because you have to. You feel completely empty and wonder if this miserable feeling will remain with you forever. Things that seemed so easy before wear you out. You feel exhausted after doing very menial tasks. There were days when I cried all day long. I started to wonder how a person would be capable of shedding so many tears. There were countless nights that I did not sleep.

You cannot be hard on yourself during this time. You have lost the single most important person in your life that you thought would remain a part of your life forever. Unfortunately that is not the case. You are left alone, vulnerable to the world around you. It can and will be hard for you to find all the pieces of your life that have scattered since they left.

There may be a point when you need to bounce back for a bit. Your friends will probably tell you when. I said for a bit, because you will go through this cycle over and over again. Each time it seems like you are not in the funk as long as you were the previous time.

Those times come back to you every now and again. Even a year after my husband was killed I have bad days. I might cry all day and then the next day I am exhausted. All I can do the next day is lie on the couch.

I began allowing myself only a few hours on these days to have a bad day. It has been very important and allows me to validate my feelings. It also keeps me moving forward and appreciating what life has given me.

You may not become okay with releasing yourself and embracing the bad times. You will know when you are having them. These are the days when you do not have the strength to face what is in front of you. These are the days when you need a friend, but would rather hide in your covers. These are the days when you need to dig down deep to find your crazy courage. Just think of it as a day or a week or a month of recharging yourself to face the world.

Use Your Crazy Courage

1. Try to let go of the guilt you may have if you have a bad day, bad week, or even a bad month.
2. You lost what was your life, give yourself a break.
3. At some point pull yourself together, look in the mirror and say, "I can join the world after a sucker punch to the face."
4. It may be difficult to embrace life right now.
5. Try to find a way to validate your feelings. Accept the encouragement your friends and family offer.
6. Remember you will shed many tears. Don't try to stop them, just let them go.

Let go and open yourself up

It was hard for me to let go and to open myself up. I was waiting for more heartache and bad things to happen to me. What changed this was meeting a few other widows and others that had lost their loved ones. It was many years after they lost their spouse or loved one and they still carried the burden of death with them. I carry the same burden and I think this is why I could recognize it. You can see the sadness in their eyes and the will to live slipping away. I vowed to myself that I would let go. I had to or I would destroy myself.

For me, the first phase was to let go of Mike's burden. I needed to begin to change from "What would Mike do?" to "What do I need to do?" I would still speak with Mike as if he were standing or sitting next to me. There was a comfort in believing that he was there to bounce my ideas off of. I thought many nights about the people I met that were lost in their grief. I wanted them to be able to look around and see life is still happening. One day I thought to myself, what would I want Mike to do if I was not here? I would want him to live and I couldn't do that myself until I let go of the burden that came with his death. I needed to get past the "if he wouldn't have gone to work that night he would still be here with us" mind set. What I needed to do is realize the truth that was right in front of my face. This happened and now I am left with all these pieces to put together. I didn't know how to put them together, but I needed to try. It was as if I was a bird flying through the sky and this glass window was in front of me. I didn't realize what it was until I flew into it and the window slapped me in the face. This feeling consumed me for months.

Slowly, I began to let go of the burden I felt for Mike and the things that he would not get to do. I began to embrace little things at first and slowly with each breath, I relieved myself of all of those burdens.

One day I was sitting in my room listening to music as I often did. I thought sometimes the music would speak to me, would bring me some signs. A song came on and I heard very vividly,' I want to celebrate my life'. Those words resonated with me. I knew that Mike was not here to celebrate the life he lived and wouldn't be able to celebrate anything. I vowed that I was going to celebrate life, because Mike couldn't. I knew that he was here with me to celebrate it. When he left, he left part of himself with me. I had an intimate bond with him and was able to send a piece of my life with him. So why not celebrate it? It was a blessing that we grew with each other creating a bond that lasted his lifetime and would last mine.

What was important is that I could let go of the notion that we would create new memories together. However, I realized that I could still keep all of the vivid memories of our life together with me. I came to recognize that I was afraid and filled with fear. I was afraid if I let go of that deep dark grief that lingered inside of me like the plague, I would be letting go of everything. I didn't have to let go of it all, I only needed to let go of my dark friend.

The relief you feel inside when you recognize this is astounding. It is difficult to describe, but it is like you have been driving down this long dark tunnel. You cannot see in front of you, to the sides or even behind you. You are blinded by the darkness that has crept all around you. You are lost until you see only a glimpse of the light at the end of the tunnel. It gives you the hope that you will not be surrounded by darkness for all of eternity. That light you see is hope, and hope brings the desire to continue. When you continue you are almost forced to let others into your life. You need to allow yourself to let go. Give yourself permission to do it.

When you open yourself up again you begin to live, to look around you. You might look out your window again and not be so angry at all those neighbors on your street deciding to live their lives. You will want to be a part of the living world and experience it all again. It will be refreshing. As if you were a small child again who has discovered an intriguing new flower and after smelling its sweet fragrances, you cannot wait to run across the next one.

Use Your Crazy Courage

1. Let go of any burden you may feel.
2. Open yourself up slowly.
3. You may get hurt again, but don't shut the world out. You may miss out on some of your life if you do.
4. Remind yourself that you are only letting go of fear, not your memories.

Listen to yourself

You may not think you know what the right answer is in any given situation, but you do. Your feeling of helplessness seems to take over and you question your ability to make good choices. Look back at your life. Did you always make the right choice? I doubt it. But those decisions brought you to where you are today and where you were with your spouse. Life is about endless decisions and we make them on a regular basis. A lot of times we do not listen to ourselves. We let others influence what we believe to be the right path. Sometimes it's not. These are decisions about what's right for you.

Others are not able to make those decisions for you. They may try very hard to manipulate you, make you feel guilty or just convince you that their opinion is the right choice. But deep down you know what you want.

When we were young our parents made those choices for us. They taught us how to act, how to be in life. They parted ways with us when we were capable of being independent. You are still capable of this. Although it might seem like you are not.

For the first several months my motto was "What would Mike do?". This helped me make good decisions. Looking back I would not change the things I did, regardless of what other people thought at the time. Mike still brought a sense of security to me, which helped me make decisions I would even have discussions with him. I knew Mike and I knew what he would say to me in various circumstances. I could play out the discussion we would have about the subject I was thinking about. I would see him sitting there looking at me, arguing his point even though he was no longer there. Mike always helped me see the other side of a situation, even if I was too blind to see it myself. We had so many discussions throughout our marriage that it was second nature to hear his side of the issue at hand.

The most important thing to do is be confident in you. Know that you have made it this far in life and you can continue to trudge through. Just think how proud you will be of yourself and how proud your spouse would be right now if you do what you know is right.

Use Your Crazy Courage

1. Listen to what your thoughts and body are telling you. Decide if it is right or wrong for you.
2. Remember that you know what to do.
3. Develop a motto if it helps.
4. Try to be confident.

You are not in control of all things

Words can't even describe how you feel. It is a clash of disbelief and knowing your life is changed forever. It is like when cold and warm air meet and creates a thunderstorm. The clouds come in and thunder, then lightening and it begins to pour rain. You are left outside with no umbrella to shield you from the rain, so you run until you reach the first shelter you can find. You wait there until the storm stops. Instead this storm continues and doesn't blow over. So you are forced out in the wet cold rain again and again. You cannot control if a storm blows in. It's similar to the fact that we cannot control everything in our lives. It is a hard concept to get in touch with. Trust me, you can ask anyone that knew me before. I had to be in control, if things were not going the way I wanted them to, I would get frustrated and try to push through until I had control again. This control was really a figment of my imagination. I thought I was in control of all aspects of my life until I got the knock on the door with the news of my husband's death. Then I realized that I cannot control it all.

This is also a gift that I received. I realized things are not forever and I am not in control of everything in my life. It has helped me really live my life. It has helped me understand how someone could wake up each day happy to be alive; not irritated about all the things they have to do in the day, but thankful they have something.

One thing you are in control of is you. We do not get to chose when we live or when we die. But we certainly get to chose to live and I mean really live our lives. We will fall down and our world is shattered, but we can chose to stand up and live again.

Use Your Crazy Courage

1. We cannot control everything.
2. We are in control of ourselves.
3. Think about the gifts you have in your life.
4. Really live your life.
5. Letting go of a little control may ease some of your stress.

Chapter Two
YOUR CHILDREN

The strength to tell them what happened

The day Mike died; one of our friends went to pick our oldest son, Quincy, up from school for me. When he came in he had a look of bewilderment on his face. His green eyes were big and distorted with concern. I took his hand and led him upstairs. His hand felt so small, like we traveled back in time and he was 2 years old again. As we walked upstairs, I knew the words I chose would be ones he would remember for the rest of his life. When we entered into my bedroom he saw my face for the first time. Before this, I had shielded my face from him. My children have always observed my facial expressions and I knew if he had seen it he would be panicked.

What he saw on my face made the life seem to leave his eyes while concern filled them. I knew these words were going to strike him and pierce his little heart. I reached down and took both of his hands in mine. Now we were facing each other. I looked deep into his eyes and felt myself leave my body. It was like I was standing next to us watching this scene. The words poured out of my mouth. "Quincy, your dad was in an accident this morning. I am sorry but your dad has died." He immediately looked confused, ripped his hands from mine and bolted out my door. I ran after him calling his name. I touched his shoulder and asked him to come back to my room. He came back. I said to him clutching his hands more sternly this time. "Do you understand what I said? Your dad is dead. I know that it may seem I was too blunt with him, but I did not think sugar coating anything would serve any purpose for him at that time.

Quincy turned onto his stomach and began to sob. He grabbed Mike's pillow and sobbed even harder into it. I had seen him cry many times in his 8 years. But this was different. It was something I could not make better. I couldn't kiss his scratch or give him any reason for what had occurred. For the first time I did not know what to do as a mother. I began to rub his back as he sobbed. I cannot say how long this lasted. Suddenly he sat up and turned the TV on. I think this was his way of tuning out what had happened for a little bit. We sat there in utter silence.

As I sat there I knew what I had to do next. I needed to pick up my youngest son from daycare. I asked a friend to drive me. We got in the car and I cannot even remember our conversation. Maybe we sat there in silence. We pulled into the driveway of the daycare. My heart sank and all of the strength I had left in me had to be used to pull myself together. I opened my door, which seemed so heavy to me. I walked up the sidewalk and rang the doorbell. Rhyan's daycare provider opened the door. I knew he had known what happened, because he had the same look of sympathy on his face as everyone else did that day. I told him I needed to get Rhyan. Rhyan came from the other room because he heard my voice. I snatched him up and gave him a hug. Rhyan was only two at the time and had no concept of what happened. I decided that I would not try to explain anything to him until he asked for his dad. Maybe this would allow one person in our family to feel normal for a little longer.

Seeing your children after you received the news that your husband had died brings another level of grieving and heartache. I am not sure how to explain it, but if you are in my shoes you know what I mean. You look at your children and think about all the firsts they are going to have in their life and think about yourself as a child. You remember your parents always being there for you. Suddenly you feel the burden of taking on all of the responsibilities of your children alone. I was a confident mother and felt that I could manage anything in their lives, but that confidence quickly left when I had to explain to two boys their father was not coming back.

My youngest son just recently asked me if his dad was in heaven. I told him yes. He said that makes him sad and he is not going to see him again. I told him that I was sad too. He asked why. I told him because we loved daddy and I miss him. We sat on the balcony, him on my lap. He looked up into the sky and pointed to it. He said my daddy is up there now. This brought tears to my eyes as his small hands reached for mine.

There are many things that will scare you, but face them. Take the opportunity to use your crazy courage. I believe once you get past the first 30 seconds you will be undefeatable.

Your children will impress you

Children bring a different perspective to things. They lost their father that was supposed to be there for them. My two sons Quincy and Rhyan are 5 years apart. They both have very distinct personalities and are polar opposites. Quincy is and has been since he was born, a laid back child. He is always content with his surroundings. Quincy is also a proud older brother that enjoys teaching his younger brother new "tricks". He is very caring and compassionate towards people. He would give anyone anything he could. He also believes everything that anyone says. He does not understand lying and thinks people are generally honest. My youngest child, Rhyan is pretty much the opposite of this. He is impatient, gets frustrated easily and thinks the world might end any given moment you tell him no. He also thinks you are very beautiful when he wants something from you. Rhyan is definitely the boss. I love both of my children deeply and appreciate their differences. If all kids were the same life would be pretty boring, wouldn't it? I can tell you they both got something from their dad and that is the love to serve and protect. The many Nerf guns that fill their bedrooms, "secret missions" they go on with the lights out in the house and their desire to get the "bad" guys is only a small way they demonstrate that to me.

Of my children, for Quincy especially, their father brought a certain sense of safety. For several months our son Quincy would ask who is going to protect us. He felt our home was a place of safety when his dad was here. Now that feeling was lost to him and he was left with so many questions. He thought his father was undefeatable and somehow he was defeated. You watch your children deal with the pain and it comes out in many ways that you weren't expecting. I have two boys at very different stages in their lives and have developed ways to support them both. It is human nature to adapt to your surroundings and you do; not immediately, but one day you will look around and see your children laughing again. The laughter will fill your heart with the joy that had been missing for so long.

The smartest thing I did with my eight year old, Quincy, was take him to a counselor. In the very beginning Quincy was angry. He would throw fits, just as if he were two years old again. I would have to hold him down so he would not hurt himself or anyone else. He was very mean to his brother and would destroy things. He turned from sweet to sour. This was from the loss he felt from his father dying, as I learned from his counselor.

A way Quincy learned to release his anger was punching a bag or even the pillows on his bed. I placed a punching bag in a room for Quincy to use when he felt these anger surges. After we got through the anger stage we continued through therapy and I would bring his little brother with him once in a while. They had him do a few things that really helped him. He was taught to understand and identify what he was feeling. This can be challenging even for some adults. In addition to this Quincy began to write in a journal. He didn't have to write in it every day, but I encouraged him to do this anytime he began having feelings about his father. I will tell you that I look through it so I know how he is feeling. There was also a time when Quincy thought he had to be the man of the house and I had to squash that immediately. He is only a child and needs to be one; I continually shared that message with him.

Rhyan was 2 when his father was killed. He had no concept of what was really happening. To this day he will randomly ask me if his father is dead or tell me his father was killed by a lady. On those days he is almost obsessed with the idea. It took me some time to feel comfortable with him talking about the incident, but I realized that his feelings needed to be validated as well. Rhyan recently became obsessed with the idea that when he gets older he will be able to fix his daddy. It is very difficult to tell him again and again that daddy cannot be saved. That there is nothing that anyone can do.

Another big impact on my children is we normally spend some time each day talking about our feelings and the fact that we miss Dad. In the beginning we did it before bed, now we bring it up randomly. I try to point out behaviors my sons share with their father. It makes them smile every time.

There were times when I was angry with my children, because I felt like they were not grieving properly. They would play with their friends and act as if nothing had happened. It took me some time and some sessions with a counselor to realize it was their way of grieving. They filled their aching hearts in ways that were much different than mine. They were children and what better way for them to heal than through play. When I felt this way towards my children I would give them a big hug or as we call them squeezie-squeezies. The embrace washed all the anger away and the perspective of how small they were came back to me.

The anger was here and there in the beginning, but what was a constant for me was how I was always impressed with my children. There were days when they helped me get out of bed and reminded me that life still needs to continue. There are stories I want to tell you about my children. These are only two things from several that I could share, but I think these two events affected me most.

One day I witnessed something that I don't believe a parent wants to see but makes you proud that you have raised your children. This was the day after Mike was killed and the house was very quiet compared to the day before. I had woken up very early in the morning right before the sun was rising; to be honest I am not sure I even slept. No one else was awake in the house so I went outside and sat on my patio crying uncontrollably, saying over and over in my head that I could not believe he was dead. My heart began to sink deep in my chest just as it had done the day before. When the sun hit the horizon it hit my face and I felt its warmth. This brought more reality and anguish that I would need to survive another day without my husband. I was not sure how I was going to be able to face anyone or our family as they arrived. I went back up to my bedroom which would give me some comfort. Lying in our bed with the smell of Mike on the pillow somehow comforted me. I laid there for some time before capturing all the strength I needed for the day. I got dressed and looked into the mirror. When I looked at myself I saw a woman with eyes glazed red from the thousands of tears that had fallen. I began to peer deeper into my eyes and saw emptiness. I didn't recognize those eyes as my own, but they were.

I began walking down the stairs only hearing the whispers of my children in the sitting room. I could not hear what they were talking about until I reached the bottom of the staircase and that is when I saw what they had in their hands. They were playing with a border patrol truck. The very same truck that Mike had given to them when he was in the patrol and an almost exact replica of what Mike was driving the day he was killed. Fear shot through my body and I was not sure if I should run, but I couldn't. My body was stiff and my legs unable to move. I was gasping for air as I heard Quincy explaining to Rhyan what has happened to their dad. Quincy began, "Dad was driving down the road and then the lady hit him. When she hit him his truck rolled over like this. This is how dad died." Rhyan asked, "Why did she hit him?" Quincy replied," Because she drank too many beers." I had not realized that Quincy knew these details, but kids do hear everything. What I was watching at that moment was a big brother sharing something with his little brother that their mother was not strong enough to explain at that moment.

I was impressed with Quincy during the funeral service. I had chosen only to bring Quincy and not to bring his little brother. During the service I cried many times. Each time I began to cry Quincy would rub my back. I never understood why he did this and was quite frustrated with myself that I did not comfort him more. I asked him recently why he rubbed my back. He told me he did it, because I was sad and crying. There were several times in his life that I had comforted him this way and didn't think he could demonstrate that behavior towards me at such a young age.

My children went through an emotional rollercoaster, just as I did. You look into their eyes and see the loss they experienced and their eyes remind you of your own. There were many times that I asked myself how am I going to be able to "fix" this feeling they have when I am not sure how to fix my own? I was still a mother and those instincts still prevail. You may be lying in bed and begin to hear the sobs coming from their room. You question if you should let them be alone in their thoughts or rush to them to comfort them. I typically played off my own mood. If I was at a point when I wanted a hug, I would go to them. I would only ask them if they wanted to talk about it. If they said no, I would not say anything except—when you are ready I am here. If they wanted to talk about it they could. Even though you are at an emotional low, you are still able to read your child's emotions.

I want you to know that if you have children they will impress you even at the most stressful times. It may be unexpected. They feel your sorrow and have their own to carry with them. What we all hope for is that they are able to take the things that we teach them and share these gifts with others.

Use Your Crazy Courage

1. It's okay if you feel angry towards your children. Take a deep breath; it will go away as you gain understanding of their grieving process.
2. Ask your children to keep a "feelings" journal if they are old enough. This journal can be helpful to them while they are working through their own emotions.

3. Talk about your feelings with your children about the death of their parent.
4. Take time each day with your children to talk about the parent they lost.
5. Your children will get you out of bed once in a while, get up and play with them.
6. Squash any thoughts they have about needing to be the man or woman of the house. They are children and need to understand they have time to grow up.
7. It's okay if your children comfort you once in a while, they learn this from you.
8. Let your children talk about what happened to the parent they lost, it will validate their thoughts and feelings.
9. Remember your children will impress you, smile because you are proud.

It is okay for your children to see you cry

I always wanted to be strong for my children, but sometimes crying together or letting them see that you are sad will make them realize that it is ok to be sad. You are your children's role model. You want them to grow up being capable of showing their emotions. I was apprehensive to cry in front of them at first. I was worried that they would see their mother lose control and feel their stability slipping away. I cried in front of them some times and what they saw was their mother sad grieving the loss of their daddy.

My son Quincy and I were talking about the subject of crying. I was telling him that crying was like a stomach ache. When you throw up you normally feel better, right? He said yes. I told him the tightness in his throat and the feeling he has inside before he cries is like a stomach ache. If he cries it will make him feel better. It was actually scientifically proven. He was delighted by this information. He told me that he thought he wasn't supposed to cry because he was a boy. I was grateful that I was able to explain this to him.

Quincy and I had some good crying sessions together. He was more comfortable crying in the comfort of his own room. When my boys go to bed each night, I like to tuck them in. This is when I would speak with

Quincy about how he was feeling. There was one night in particular that he was rather upset. He said that he missed his dad. I told him that I missed him to. I sat on the edge of his bed looking down at his innocent face watching his tears roll down his cheeks. I began to cry with him.

There were moments that reminded us of his father and that made us cry. We cried because we loved his father. The tears that we shed were for the memories of times we had with him and ones that we wouldn't forget.

Often when Quincy slept he would cry in his sleep. I would hear him down the hallway and walk into his room. He would be sound asleep, yet crying. He would make a whimpering noise that sounded like a puppy that lost its mother. These cries were hard to hear. I would sit in his room saying everything will be alright and rub his back.

Moments with Rhyan were much different. I did not sleep much and would find myself visiting my boys' rooms at night. I would check on them. Some nights I would sit with Rhyan and I would cry. I would cry, because I was not sure if he would remember his father when he got older. I cannot remember when I was two years old, nearly three. How was he going to remember his Dad? I would sit in the dark unsure of how to handle the many years of Rhyan's life without his father. I remember the look on Mike's face when he became a father and the way Mike had constantly carried Rhyan around the house when he was a baby. It sort of irritated me, because when Mike was not there Rhyan wanted held. Mike would not be there to give the guidance he had given Quincy. Then I would worry about the times that Quincy would miss with his dad. These thoughts brought tears of worry.

Rhyan would cry for his dad, when we would drive in the car. For a few weeks Rhyan did not sleep well. He did feel the pain of the loss of his father, but was not yet able to understand it fully. I cried many times he asked for his dad. Rhyan would look up at me with his big blue eyes and ask why I was crying. I would say to him that I am sad, because daddy died.

Crying with your children can help your own healing. You are continuing to build the bond with your children as you did before. It is just in a different way than you might have imagined. Let your children see you cry and cry with them.

I asked Quincy one day, if he could teach a kid his age a lesson, what would he teach them? He said that he would teach them that it is okay to cry. We can all learn a lesson from my nine year old . . . cry.

Use Your Crazy Courage

1. Cry with your children, they will not think you are unstable. You are showing them it is okay to cry.
2. Continue to be your children's role model. They will emulate your behavior.
3. Make yourself available to your children and make sure they know you are available whenever they need you.
4. Let yourself and your children continue to heal by crying with them.

Chapter Three

THE FUNERAL

Funeral

In the days before the funeral, I held onto hope that Mike may not really be dead. When I saw him lying in the casket it brought a small dose of reality except I got to look at him and touch him still. Even though his body was hard and cold, it still provided some sort of comfort to me. When I heard his star number being called out and he did not answer, I knew he was really gone. He would have never have not answered the call. He loved serving his country almost as much as he loved his family. The day he died, when his shift was over, he was speaking to fellow agents about what they had done that night when they heard the call for support from other agents some 30 miles away. Mike went to provide what support he could in apprehending the illegals. They apprehended them before he left to drive back to the station and come home. Except he didn't make it home, he didn't even make it 5 minutes up the road before he was killed. Seeing his uncles, friends and nephew carry his body back to the hearse with tear filled eyes, I knew he was not going to return. His body was in that casket and the hearse was driving it away to be cremated. He got his last wish and that was to be cremated. He would not be returning to me and I would only see his face again in my dreams and pictures. I was not sitting there in some sort of twisted dream. Knowing all of these truths, made his death a reality.

As just one single person we are very small in this world, but our decisions affect more than we know. I sat in a room full of hundreds of people not even noticing who was around me. I only saw a blur of colors that surrounded me. My husband was a comrade to so many men and women in the green uniform of the U.S. Border Patrol. He was looked up to by others. It is funny to me that he did his job every day not knowing this. I stood by unaware as well. As a wife of an agent you know all the risks your husband takes each day. But you really don't think it's going to happen to you. Then it does and you become a part of a group that you don't want to be a part of and at the same time you are proud of.

I looked forward at my husband's casket as the funeral director pulled him out of the hearse. Seeing this brought tears to my eyes and I clutched my son Quincy's shoulders even harder. My husband was lying inside of that box, lifeless. Is this where life leads? We live and then we die . . . without saying good bye. Not even knowing that these are our last moments. I didn't get to touch his hand or his face another time. I didn't feel his lips to mine. Yet, I told myself to stay strong. Mike needed me to be strong and so did my family. As the honor guard rolled Mike's casket into the church, I felt my legs following it, as if wrapped around my waist was a rope that was attached to Mike still. I only saw the aisle in front of me with the casket. I did not dare to look to either side of me, for it would bring more tears to my eyes. My heart began to race and I felt as if I were going to vomit. However, I forced myself to keep "my face on". I only had a few more rows now before I could sit.

I saw the pictures of Mike with us, his family in the front of the room. The Christmas picture stands out and it was yet another reminder that we would never spend another Christmas together. I took my seat, but kept my sunglasses on with a tear filled tissue in my hand. On one side of me was Julie and on the other, my son Quincy. As I sat there listening to the words that people had to say about my husband, one thing that I heard over and over was love. Mike and I shared love; we loved each other and believed in each other. We had something that some people do not even find in life. I was lucky to have had those moments with him.

I heard Julie speak about her brother, how she was so proud of him. He looked up to her and she was pleased to call him her brother. I heard Mike's life story coming from her shaky voice. It was with disbelief that I heard his story and the fact that his story was over. Our life together had ended.

My son leaned into me, clutching my arm. He whispered in my ear to take my sunglasses off. He was right. So I took them off of my face. He looked at me and saw the tears that my sunglasses hid. He began to rub my back. It felt very awkward, yet soothing to have my eight year old trying to comfort me.

There were two other speeches that pulled my attention away from my own internal thoughts. I heard the words of Mike's classmates and looked at them all standing on the stage with their brother in the casket in front of them. They were feeling despair. Mike was a leader to some of them. He would be missed by all of his brothers in green and as I turned my head I saw the room flooded in green uniforms. They were there to support Mike's family when he was unable to do that himself. His high school friends went to the podium to share their memories together. Mike had moved away from his friends to join the army, yet they stayed close to Mike over the years. Mike was a person you didn't want to lose touch with. He brought so much to your life that it was impossible to forget him. There were additional speakers that talked about the honor Mike carried with him each day.

Then we were signaled to leave the church. I once again followed my husband's casket. With Julie by my side we grabbed each other's hands to provide some comfort to one another. As we left the church we entered our vehicles. I needed to use the restroom. As I reentered the building I put my head down a little, hoping people wouldn't recognize me. How silly that was when they all just saw me in the church. I waited in line and people noticed. They looked at me and one woman shared her condolences. Only I didn't want to talk to anyone. I did my best to look guarded in hopes that people would get the message. I left the bathroom and went back into the car.

We began the processional. As we traveled down the roads that I had been on so many times before, I saw people lined in the streets. I saw some taking pictures and some people just watching. There was one man that I can remember distinctly. We were on the road that would take us to the cemetery. On the side of the road an older gentleman with a veteran's hat stood there at a position of attention and saluted the hearse as Mike's body passed by. He was a lone man in the middle of a field on the side of the road. He must have taken the time to make sure he was there at that fleeting moment. It brings tears to my eyes just thinking about it. At that moment I knew, Mike would forever be honored. We arrived at the cemetery and I saw the fire trucks with the American flag that we would drive through. I thought that I would only see this in movies, but no it was done for my husband.

We pulled up to the grave site and I saw the chairs lined up for the family. We sat there waiting for most of the cars to arrive and for the first time, I think we all noticed how many people really came to Mike's funeral. As we got out of the vehicle we waited for the honor guard to pull Mike's casket from the hearse, once more. The honor guard was truly amazing. Although under pressure, their precise movements were infallible. At that moment I looked around and realized I was the wife of a special man; a man that was honored for his life and service. He was going to receive honors. As we sat there in the sun, Quincy sitting next to me, we watched the honor guard fold the flag that had rested over Mike's casket. It was a beautiful site to see. They brought the flag to me and I clutched it in my hands with my son's small hand on my shoulder. I said to myself this is it. He will be leaving me today and I will not be able to run my hands through his hair again. Then the sounds of gunfire, made me jump from my thoughts, as they fired volley shots to salute him. I saw the rider less horse galloping by to honor Mike for his service. When I heard the ladies voice doing last call over the radio, his star number being called out one more time; it started becoming reality that he was not returning. He didn't answer his star number and he was a man that would never miss the opportunity to serve. Taps began to play and we were leaving the cemetery. I watched Mike's body being carried away now by his family. He would enter the hearse one more time and be cremated. His life story was now finished and I was left behind.

We began to drive towards my house where I left our youngest son, Rhyan. I chose not to take him that day. I felt he was too young at two years old. I did not believe he would have gotten anything out of it. I knew that I would not have been able to console him during the funeral. It is each person's decision on what to expose their children to and I had made mine.

Use Your Crazy Courage

1. The funeral is going to happen, so prepare yourself to see the world. Consider giving yourself alone time before the funeral. Try to rally support to help you get ready for the day (someone to watch children, help you get ready, drive you etc.).
2. Remember this funeral is for you as much as it is for your spouse, you need to say goodbye.

3. Make sure you take the time to be alone to decompress after the funeral service.
4. Take a tissue box with you.
5. Drink plenty of water. Your body needs to be fully hydrated to support your emotional state.
6. If you do not have the strength to speak don't feel obligated to talk to everyone.
7. If you get into a conversation you do not want to be in, politely excuse yourself.

You are ultimately in charge

Mike and I shared the most intimate bond and I was the person who knew him best. That is likely true in your case. You know your spouse. Remember the long nights lying next to each other in bed talking about your dreams, things you shouldn't have done and what is important in your lives; your ability to be honest with one another. The trust you put into one another. The deep secrets you share. They know what scared you most and they stood by protecting you. These are the ways you got to know your spouse and the intimate moments you shared together. Don't let other people try to pressure you into things that you know your spouse would have never wanted.

Remember when you were small and school officials used to tell you to say no to drugs? They told you not to give into peer pressure. Well, I am telling you to say no to what you know is not right.

It was difficult to plan the funeral of my husband. It will likely be one of the hardest things I will ever be forced to do. Fortunately, Mike and I had that conversation about what he would want. I did not know everything and we never put a will in place. We thought we were too young to have to worry about it. I knew he wanted to be cremated. That was certain. A few months before his death he was talking about how he was unsure about being cremated, then one day he came home from work and said he definitely wanted to be. Another request he had for me was to keep his ashes in an urn next to my bed. He did not give me a timeframe, but I still have them on a shelf in my room. One day when I know where to bury him, I will. During the funeral planning I made my opinion known to the funeral director and at one point actually yelled at him. Probably not the kindest gesture I have ever done, but I knew what needed to happen for the funeral and he was trying to tell me something wasn't possible. Well it was and it happened at the funeral.

After Mike died, I was worried about a will. My children did not have a father any longer and if something happened to me I was not sure what would happen to them. So I had a will put in place. I did it quickly, but the most important thing to me was to know that my children would be taken care of. You are now the sole parent for your children. It is you that is in charge of taking care of them. You decide what is best for your children. You can ask for advice, but it is your decision. You will also have financial decisions to make. There will be many more things to decide. Remember you are in charge. This is your life.

I can say I was lucky with our family. No one argued with any decisions that were made. But I do know other widows that have horror stories about their families. Their families would try to take over. Not letting the widow be in charge. This is completely unfair and should not happen. Remember that you have all the control in the situation. You shared a bond that will carry you through the years.

Use Your Crazy Courage

1. Share your thoughts and feelings even if you are unsure whether or not you should.
2. This is a time in your life when you are very vulnerable. Do not give into peer pressure, and the expectations of others. People may try to take advantage of you, if you think they are stop them quickly.
3. Remember this is your life and you are in charge of it.
4. Do what is critical right now and worry about the small stuff later.
5. Write a list of what you need to do, if you can't do it all find a way to delegate responsibilities.
6. People may try to take advantage of you. Recognize when this may be happening and put a stop to it.

Hard choices don't cease after the funeral

We would all hope that after burying your spouse, your hard choices would be over. Unfortunately this is not the case. If you have children, there are many things you need to decide. You need to decide when they should go back to school. Do you stay at home with your little ones who aren't yet in school? Maybe you need to figure out how you are going to afford to pay for those bills that are lingering. All of these decisions seem even more difficult than they were before. I have only listed a very small percentage of decisions that you are going to need to make.

On December 2nd, 2010, I received a call from my family. They informed me that my grandmother had died suddenly of a heart attack. This was exactly 3 months after my husband was killed. I felt as if my struggles were never ending. My grandmother became a widow at a young age as well. She lost my grandfather in an accident. My uncle was only six when he died. She faced the similar trauma I was facing now. I spoke with her only a few weeks before. She understood what I was going through and was doing her best to comfort me. She was able to relate with me and provide me with a bit of crazy courage.

The next day my children and I boarded a plane to my childhood home for my grandmother's funeral. Hours after arriving, I received a phone call informing me there would be a hearing to determine if the accused drunk driver that crashed into Mike's service vehicle would stay in custody or be released until trial. They asked if I would be able to speak as the victim, but I couldn't be in two places at once. This would give me the opportunity to share with the judge how the drunk driver's actions had impacted the lives of my children and myself. The words that I spoke could influence the judge's decision to keep the accused detained until trial. The hearing was set for the very same time of my grandmother's funeral. My mind was reeling with the dilemma that I now faced. Should I stay for the funeral or should I attend the hearing? After speaking to family members, guilt ridden I decided to stay for my grandmother's funeral. Given the circumstances, I believe there was no right decision but my torment was lessened due to the knowledge that my sister-in-law was there to speak on my family's behalf at the hearing. During my grandmother's funeral I decided to recite a poem. To me it was as if I was speaking to both my grandmother and Mike.

Here is the poem I read . . .

You never said "I'm leaving"
You never said goodbye
You were gone before I knew it
And only God knows why

A million times I needed you,
A million times I cried,
If love alone could have saved you,
You never would have died.

In life I loved you dearly,
In death I love you still,
In my heart you hold a place,
That no one could ever fill.

It broke my heart to lose you,
But you didn't go alone,
For part of me went with you.
The day God took you home.

-Unknown

I was not capable of speaking at Mike's funeral. I wish I had the strength to do it then, but I did not. At the same time I was reading this poem, my sister-in-law was speaking in court facing the accused. It is really bizarre how that worked out. After the funeral I waited for the call on the decision to keep the accused detained or released until trial. The judge ruled to allow her to be released. I felt instant guilt. I thought I was letting Mike down again. I was not able to be there for him as he was dying, holding his hand or rubbing my fingers through his hair. I wasn't able to tell him I loved him. An appeal was quickly filed and there would be another hearing a couple of days after I returned, but it didn't take away any guilt. I was able to be distracted for a couple of days with family affairs. In my down moments I began writing a letter to the judge for the appeal hearing. Thankfully I had my sister Stacy who provided me with rational assistance. I was an emotional mess.

As I returned home I thought about the days that preceded and the days that were to follow after we buried my grandmother. I continued to prepare for my statement in court in the days that followed.

The days went by quickly and it was the day that I would speak in court to determine if the ruling would be overturned. Seeing the accused made my blood boil. It is anger that I was unable to control. I hope one day that I will be able to get over this anger towards her. I am not sure if I will. The anxiety of hearing her lawyer speak was worse than I had ever experienced. Her lawyer reminded me of a used car salesman that just so happened to resemble Joe Dirt. I am not sure if I was even listening to the words he said, only to his voice. I was waiting my turn to speak and was watching for my cue. Then it came and now I was going to walk up to the podium to share how this had impacted my life. There was no way to say it in words, but I wrote it out and hoped it would serve its purpose. I felt the pressure, if what I was going to say did not impact the judge enough than they would let her out into the world until she went to trial. As I walked up to the podium I looked straight ahead at the judge. I stood there for a moment shaking uncontrollably and felt the tightness in my throat. My tears began to run down my cheeks and I hadn't even started to speak. I took a few more moments to collect myself and began.

After I read my statement I gathered my papers and walked back to my seat. I was not capable of looking at the accused. I was worried I would be unable to control my emotions if I looked at her face. I waited for the judge to make his ruling. He ruled that day to keep her in prison until her trial. I left the court room feeling as if I had comforted Mike in some small way by preventing the accused from leaving jail until the trial.

Another decision I made was to meet with the head EMT and investigator of Mike's crash. I didn't have to meet with them, but I needed to know that everything was done properly. I was able to read the reports and see only a few pictures. I did see his vehicle that day as well. It was covered with a black tarp. I was not able to go near it because it was still classified as evidence. I did uncover a few things that I did not know that day. It did not make me sleep any better, but it answered a lot of questions I had that raced through my mind on a regular basis. I thought hearing these facts would stop all of the scenarios of the crash running through my mind. It stopped the many scenarios but now the facts replaced them; like thousands of termites eating away slowly at the structure of a home.

I did not cry that day when I was speaking with the two men. I saved it all for that night, alone in the darkness of my room, curled up in a corner.

Decisions that need to be made are ongoing. We have to pull ourselves together and face those decisions head on. We may not always make the best decisions, but we are capable of making them. If you need help ask someone's opinion about it. Just remember some decision may affect you for the rest of your life, so think before you act.

Use Your Crazy Courage

1. You might think things will get easier after the funeral. They may not. Be patient.
2. Ask others that you trust about the decisions you need to make, listen to their opinions but you should ultimately decide what is best for you.
3. Remember you are capable of making decisions.
4. Don't avoid those immediate decisions that you will to need to make. There will be relief in taking them on.
5. If a choice is hard to make and isn't immediate, be patient and make sure you know all of your options.
6. You may need to let others down, just don't let yourself down.

The gift of money

The gift of money after your spouse dies can be a tradeoff that you do not want. People and organizations give you money to help, even accepting the life insurance was challenging for me to stomach. The gifts and money I received made me feel like I traded my spouse for a paycheck. I thought that maybe if I didn't take it he might come back. Then reality set in and I looked around to see that I had two kids to take care of for the rest of my life. To me, it felt like Mike was still there taking care of his family, taking care of us.

It was the very first day after Mike's death and the chaplain told me that there was someone at the door to give me something. I was very hesitant to go and told him I didn't know if I wanted to. Then I looked over to one of our friends and he shook his head yes as if he knew what I was thinking. I went to the door and there were two men there to present me with a check. This happened several times over the first year. I was grateful because these donations helped me survive financially for several months.

Every time I received a gift it made me cry. I am not sure why, but it did. It also brought a feeling of nausea with it. This is definitely the tradeoff that you do not want.

There are several things that you need to think about when you consider your finances. It may be difficult, but this is where you need to try to take the emotion out of it.

In my situation, I am sure like many others, we did not have a will. Being Mike's wife made me the next of kin and made everything a little less complicated to deal with. However finances are very complicated, especially if you were not the one that had to worry about them when your spouse was alive. The first thing you might want to do is consult with a financial advisor once you gather all of the financial information. Sometimes your bank will give you a free financial consultation.

You will need several things in hand: death certificate (get at least 10 copies), marriage certificate, birth certificates, and social security information. Another bit of information for you is that bill collectors don't care that you are grieving. There might be bills that were only in your spouse's name. If that is the case, negotiate with them. They may ask you if it has gone through probate. I am not going to even try to explain that to you, but I advise calling a legal representative to explain it to you. If bill collectors call you and send you bills to the estate of your spouse's name, hold off on speaking to them until the financial aspects get worked out. This is also a time when legal advice will help.

I had to provide my bank a letter of testimony for a specific account. This is actually easy to obtain from the local court house. You will just need to provide proof you were their spouse, which can be done with the marriage certificate.

There are many people you will work with such as employee benefits, social security administration, lien holders, other creditors, post office, utility companies and many more. You want to notify certain places immediately and others can wait. The hardest thing that I did was changing my bank accounts into my name and taking his off. It was another reminder that he was gone.

Finances are difficult to manage even when your spouse was alive. Take some time and make sure you are able to understand what all of the institutions tell you. If not, ask a friend to help you. Trust me, not everyone is looking out for your best interests. Money is cold and not grieving.

Use Your Crazy Courage

1. Gather all financial information.
2. Obtain at least 10 copies of the death certificate.
3. Gather information such as birth certificates, marriage license, and social security information.
4. Consult with a financial advisor if possible.
5. Get legal counsel if you can.
6. Finances can be confusing, so ask for help when needed.

Chapter Four

THE PEOPLE YOU MEET AND THE PEOPLE YOU KNOW

The people you meet

We meet people every day that say things that inspire us. It could be something very profound and that moves us forward in our lives. There are also people that are out in this big world that we may never meet or are unaware they even exist but who have a lot of insight. Through this tragedy I was able to meet some of the most amazing people I now have in my life.

Until something of this magnitude strikes you, you may have never met them. There was a generosity that I never knew about until September 2nd, 2010. It came from all around me. Family, friends, neighbors and even organizations that I wish I would have paid closer attention to before. We are in the tunnel of life so often that we don't see what is around us. I received many gifts and they were not all of monetary value. I am not sure if it is the emotional level that you get to that allows you to really appreciate these people or if people change when they know you need them. I hope this love surrounds anyone that must experience such a loss.

I have to say one gift that I got out of this tragedy, was the people that surround me now. If you are sitting there wondering where those people are in your life, search for them.

There is one friend that I would have likely never met, unless September 2nd had happened. He was the man in the black shirt with the notebook in his hand the morning I received the news of Mike's death. He is a chaplain. He stood by my family's side during this first year. He was there when I heard the news and there when I was getting frustrated with the funeral director. He observed me and began to understand my cues very quickly. We have had countless conversations and never has he judged me. There was one day in particular that I can remember the most. I was explaining to him how angry I was at God. I had been trying to figure out for some time why God had chosen to take Mike that day. What did I do wrong to cause this to happen and why would he let evil prevail? I couldn't even pray at the time, because I felt that God didn't have my respect anymore. What the chaplain said to me that day made me understand religion more than I have in my whole life. He said God isn't about good prevailing over evil. What it is truly about is having a relationship with God. This single comment from the chaplain took away a lot of anger I had. It wasn't immediate; I pondered that message the whole day. That night after the kids went to bed, I sat outside on the patio looking up at the sky and thought to myself: *if you are really up there then hear what I am about to say.* I reached my hands out and warm tears ran down my face. This time it wasn't really tears of sadness but tears of hope. I said, *please God take care of Mike for me, you know I am not able to and I made a promise to Mike that I would. He is with you now.*

That night I was able to get up and walk up the stairs to my bedroom with a little bit of comfort. Something that had completely disappeared from my life and this one moment was able to start to bring it back.

I found myself intrigued with trying to connect with Mike on a spiritual level after this. I just didn't want to admit it, because of the anger I felt towards God. I would sit in my room late at night feeling like Mike was there. I would talk to him, sometimes for hours. I asked him what I should do and asked for his guidance. It was truly a one sided conversation, but I would always look for signs of him answering me the days that followed. At times, I would dream we were together and talking about what I had asked him before I fell asleep. One night I vividly remember when I asked him to tell me it was okay for me to move on with my life. To begin a life that didn't involve him. He is and will always be a part of my life; he just holds a different place now, in my memories. That very night I dreamt that we were walking and stopped next to this giant tree. I told him my feelings and he looked at me. He told me not to worry about all the little stuff and said he gave me permission to start my life again. I cried in my dream and I woke up with tears on my cheeks.

There was another person I met that first month. It was someone I had known since she was born. I shared a bedroom with her growing up and had been through many trial and tribulations with her. It was my little sister. I thought I knew her so well. But this is when I met a different side of her. I was the one that she had come to for advice; I had taken care of her for many years. This was different for me; I needed her to take care of me. I needed her to be in control of everything like I had so many times before. I was her big sister and it was my responsibility to care for her. She came the very same day Mike was killed. She dropped everything, I mean literally walked out of work telling them she needed to go now. From the moment she walked in the door of my house that day, she was in charge of my life for a little while. She made sure everything was done the way that I would want it done and took a lot of the burden from me. She even fielded my phone calls. She took charge and man was she good at it. I want you to know that you will meet new people you have never met before and you will meet new sides of people that you haven't seen before.

Yet I had other familiar people by my side. They are consistent people to me. My older sister Stacy is one of those people. I met her many years ago; well she met me when I was born. She is one of the most practical people I know. She is always realistic and can keep me focused and grounded. She has a way of being able to look at the big picture and seeing all of the little pieces that go with it as well. She is a person that can analyze the details when you are incapable of doing so. She is conscious of my feelings, but I don't think she is afraid to hurt them either. Well I am not afraid to hurt hers, because she is my sister and I know she understands me. Sometimes you need to hear something in a direct manner with no sugar coating. That is how we are able to talk to each other. We are able to really talk and have a conversation. We can forget all of the meaningless pieces of a conversation and be who we are. I have been able to always depend on her and still can. She is here for me one authentic conversation at a time.

There are several ways to find people that you might need right now. I suggest you find a support group for young widows or find blogs on the internet to join, if you do not have the other support you need. Blogs keep everything a little more anonymous if you need that. One big impact on my life was finding a widow that lived in the area I was in and asking her for help. She was much wiser than I was, because she had been through what I was going through now. When I knew something was coming up or I was unsure about what to do, I would ask her what she did. She had some great advice that I will always cherish.

Many people come into our lives and teach us lessons that will never be forgotten. You should know that some of them are gifts to be grateful for. You will not know how they will help you until the time comes that they do.

Use Your Crazy Courage

1. You will meet some amazing people that will help you heal.
2. You may not even know them at the time, but keep listening.
3. It's okay to talk to your late spouse, I do.
4. Find a support group.
5. Look for widow support blogs to join.
6. Meet other widows.

Everybody has a different story or view of who your spouse was

Enjoy the many stories that people have to share about your spouse, but realize these stories may not be how your spouse actually was. However, there is no harm in letting people hold onto their point of view. People may come up to you wanting to share their stories about your spouse. I should say they will come to you with stories.

I have heard some really great stories about Mike in the last year. Some of them I have never heard before. At times, I have had people ask me what Mike thought about them and I can only share what I know. Know there are some opinions that are better left unsaid. I heard countless stories about Mike when he was working. They would say how he was always there to back them up. I listened to his sisters' share how they would tease Mike or how he would tease them. It's a story that Mike used to talk about, when he would chase one of his sisters with a feather when they were young. His other sister he would tease about a picture they took when they were older. His parents' memories of when he was growing up. My favorite story I heard was how much he loved me and the boys.

When someone dies others may want to know what place they had in that person's life. If you just listen to them and share the positive knowledge that you have about them it will give them something to hold onto. They need memories of them just as much as you do. Those memories may not play such an important role in their lives as it does yours, but it's worth it. After Mike died, it really gave me a perspective of how people change through the course of their lives. You do not realize that you change but you do. The people that knew Mike as a young child, in high school, in the army or sometime during his adult life all seemed to have different types of stories to share. I can say they all had a few common things to say about him, some traits that Mike had throughout his life. He was a man of honor, integrity and love. Everyone perceives their relationships with people on their own terms.

I learned this lesson in the countless conversations that I had with people. It was like I was meeting Mike again for the first time. Mike did share a lot about his past with me, but it was through his eyes that I knew about these stories. For the first time, I was gaining a new perspective.

Now when I speak with my children about relationship, I think it is important for them to understand how people change and their point of view may not be the same as others.

Use Your Crazy Courage

1. You might find out something new about your spouse. Listen!
2. Let people believe their perception of your spouse. It is something they need to hold onto just like you do.
3. If people ask what your spouse thought of them, share the positive.
4. Remember, it can be refreshing to hear stories about your spouse before you met each other.

The one constant thing people will bring is food

I think this is a blessing in disguise. For a long time I did not feel hungry or could even remember to eat. But then another casserole arrives for which you are thankful. Trust me you still need food.

It got to the point where we literally could not fit any more food in the refrigerator or freezer. It felt like we had gone to Dinners Done Right for a month straight. I had Tupperware with sticky notes telling us what temperature to cook it at, how long and what it was. I am very grateful for all of the food, there were some things that fell through the cracks during the first month, but luckily, food was not one of them. I am sure I did not have to cook a thing for a good three weeks.

I think there are two sides of eating when you are grieving. Either you can't eat enough or you do not want to eat at all.

My oldest son started to binge eat after he lost his father. He would sneak food into his bedroom in the middle of the night. I would find containers and empty wrappers hidden in all sorts of places. I even found food stuffed in his pillow. He wanted to fill his emptiness with food. This is very normal for a person. We all have our comfort foods we eat when we are down. It is easy to fill our void with those foods. When we feel our emptiness is a hole dug to China, we try to eat enough to stuff it with food. We want to get rid of the empty feeling any way we can. We really need to get in touch with those feelings so we are capable of healing.

I was not able to eat. Even a bit of a sandwich made me feel sick. It took me about a week before I could even eat what I would consider a meal. This was the opposite of my son, but is normal as well.

So all of those meals that get delivered are just what you need and not what you asked for. If you have people around you that are asking to help and you are not sure what to ask them for, ask them to make a meal for you. Make sure you can freeze it. You may not eat much, but you will appreciate the convenience of pre made dinners.

Use Your Crazy Courage

1. You need food, your body needs energy.
2. Try to remember to eat, even if you have to set a timer.
3. You might have a freezer full of food, be thankful for the love and support.

Everyone has an opinion

I think the saying is: *if I had a dime for every time someone says something than I would be a rich woman.* This would be the truth for as many times as people give you their opinion about what you should do or even how you should act. I learned early to take what they say and put it to the side. I will tell you that I did ask a lot of my close family and friends for their opinions about what to do. These people I would listen to and at least weigh their opinion. They should be people you trust.

There are a few pieces of good advice I received. Those few things are: He's dead and not coming back. Don't worry about anything right now. Stay lost for a while if you want to and because you can. It may sound harsh for someone to say he's dead and not coming back, but it's not. I have a friend that has listened to me for hours and hours. There is one thing she would always say to me when I would talk or act like Mike was coming back. She would say . . . "but Samantha, he's dead and not coming back." I cannot tell you how many times she said it to me. She probably should have gotten a button made with that quote on it. I don't know if she realized it, but it helped me accept the fact that he was dead and allowed me to try to move on with my life.

A family member would tell me to stop worrying about that now. I would begin to stress myself out, because I thought I had to take care of everything now. She would say to me, "Don't even worry about it now. There is plenty of time to do it later." She made me stop and think about how critical it was to do it at this given moment. Most of the time she was right and this eliminated a lot of the anxiety I had.

Another piece of valuable advice I received was: be lost for a while. There was a point when I thought I had to know where I was and what I was going to do. I believe a lot of this came from the opinions and advice everyone shared with me or even the questions people would ask me. One day I was in my counselor's office and I was telling her how I didn't know the answers to these simple questions people had for me and I was angry with myself. She looked at me and said, "It is okay . . . be lost for a while." She said if they ask you just look at them and tell them you are choosing to be lost for a while and when you decide differently you will let them know. This bit of advice put a smile on my face when I left her office that day.

There is another friend that would reply to me quite often, "Because you can." I would often question my decisions or ask myself why would I do that? Even when the decision I was making was perfectly acceptable, she would look at me and say, "Because you can." We finally got to a point that makes me laugh just thinking about it. She would say, "You know why?" and I would reply, "Because I can." What she probably doesn't know is that when I question myself now, I say in my head, *because I can*. This was another moment of validation for me. It allowed me to gain confidence in my own decisions.

The opinions people share with you are frustrating at certain moments and when they are, walk away or run if you need to. Sometimes I would smile at people giving this advice and just watch their lips move ignoring all the words that came out. You will learn very quickly what makes you angry. It's like bomb sitting inside you waiting to explode. You begin to feel very warm, your heart starts to pound and your eyes look straight at their jugular. You think to yourself: why the hell are you saying that to me right now? When this happens take a deep breath, rationalize your feelings by telling yourself you are too emotional to deal with this advice right now. Then interrupt them, tell them thanks but you do not want to talk about that right now and walk away. Trust me they will not think anything of it. They will blame it on your emotional imbalances.

After Mike was killed there were several social media sites that were filled with various messages and my own began to fill up with the same messages. I am not sure when I read them all, but at one point or another I did. There was one message that I read somewhere that really pissed me off. The message said something like he is in a better place. I am sorry but you do not tell a person (not knowing their religious beliefs) that their husband and son's father is in a better place. Where we believed the best place for Mike was, was with us.

There were a few more things that caused instant anger for me. One was when people tried to tell me how to raise my children or things I need to do differently (unless I asked them for the advice of course) and the other was when they would say they felt sorry for me. I don't understand what would possess them to give parental advice even when they do not have any children. And what made me incapable of making those decisions now? And please do not feel sorry for me, you can empathize with me. Try to put yourself in my shoes and try to figure out how I might feel before opening your mouth. If you cannot even manage to understand how I might feel then say I am sorry about your loss. Not I feel sorry for you. If you cannot bring yourself to say anything just give a nod. That is truly enough.

A bit of advice I would give someone that is interacting with someone that has had a loss: stop talking and listen. They are not at any emotional level to process what you are saying. If you want to be a resource for them to use, listening is the best way. It does need to be a two way conversation, but if you were not that close with them before the incident it will be hard for them to respect your feelings of loss on top of what they are feeling.

Sometimes you may feel that you might be able to make a connection if you talk about your own feelings, but you won't. It will create anger inside of the widow that will cause them to keep you at a distance.

I remember when I met a particular widow a few months after Mike was killed. I was a little nervous, because I was not ready to hear about her loss. I was not able to grieve for her with my own grief still so new. What she did that day was listen. She put her emotions aside and was able to talk to me about my own. This made me feel very important and I think about that often. I only hope that I am able to do this for another person as it was done for me.

What you should remember is that someone's opinion is theirs, not yours. Everyone has the right to their opinion. A lot of opinions come from their own personal judgments. Let those people judge away. They will judge you if you do what's right or even what's wrong. You are the only one that will determine if it is right or wrong. Your actions will likely have no impact on their lives. What you need to do right now is be selfish, even if it is for the first time in your life.

Use Your Crazy Courage

1. Take a deep breath when you find you are getting angry with someone's advice or opinion. Tell them you do not feel like talking about it and walk away.
2. Some people do give good advice, sometimes you need to open up your mind to it.
3. Distance yourself from those people who aren't helping.
4. Keep your close friends by your side.
5. Ask others to listen to you.
6. If you feel compelled to, let those people that give you good advice give it to you, then thank them, but know you don't need to act on any piece of advice.
7. Sometimes you don't realize you're getting good advice until days, weeks, or months after you hear it.
8. Be selfish when you need to be.

People don't know what to say

People can say or do the most unexpected things, because they don't know what else to do. Let's just say they likely don't have practice with this sort of things. Let's just say that they are naive. This is why we need to forgive them for what they do not know. I wasn't sure what to say so how could I expect them to know? But in the same breath I could be angry at their social incompetence. I want to tell you a couple of stories of when I encountered people that didn't know what to say. I can laugh now, but at the time I was furious.

After the funeral I had a gathering at my home for everyone to come together. There was a woman at my home the entire day that I did not know. I watched her throughout the day, because she was a little loud and would glance at me once in a while. I had no idea who she was and it seemed a little unorthodox. After the long day, night had fallen and I was exhausted. I was sitting outside on my patio with a few family members. This woman happened to walk outside and started some small talk. Then she bent down to me and reached her hand out. She said, "Hi, I haven't met you yet. What is your name?" I might have said to her: *Do you realize you have been in my house all day and you were at my husband's funeral and now you are asking who I am?* I didn't say anything, but my name. I didn't have the energy, nor did I want to punish her for not knowing what to say. There is a high likelihood that she knew who I was, but she didn't know how to approach me.

Another frustrating thing people did was try to explain how they knew me. It felt like they were saying, *I know you because of my cousin's brother's sister's husband.* This had no pertinence to the situation even if they wanted to give their condolences. It was important that they were there to give their support. It was irrelevant how they knew me.

The last instance that I will share with you was attending my son's sports events. We lived in a small enough community that everyone knew what had happened, not to mention news like this spreads like wildfire. I remember sitting at the first practice I attended after my husband's death. I would see the stares from people around me. At first I felt like maybe I was being a little paranoid, but my family that came with me noticed it as well. I was unsure what to do or say to them. It was completely uncomfortable. A lot of people took the opposite approach; instead of trying to say something they said nothing at all. I cannot tell you what is worse. These were the parents that a few weeks before I had been laughing with and my husband had spoken to. What I believe had happened was fear had consumed them.

One day after receiving some valuable advice, I walked up to the parents at practice and started a casual conversation with them. I said, "The boys are starting to look good." This started a conversation that people were scared to have. Sometimes we need to make it comfortable for others.

If people don't know what to say, they should just tell us that, it would save a lot of frustration, but that is not going to happen. Just expect there will be someone that will not know what to say. Would you know what to say in the moments after a tragedy like this?

Use Your Crazy Courage

1. Forgive people with social incompetence.
2. If people are looking at you, walk up to them and talk about the weather. They likely don't know what to say.
3. People don't know how to relate to you and that is okay.
4. You may become frustrated with people's comments. Think it through and take a deep breath before replying.
5. You will very like experience someone saying the "wrong" thing. Let it go.
6. Remember that strangers may try to explain how they know you.

Appearances can be deceiving

I used to assume when women talked to me about their kids and they weren't wearing a ring, they were divorced. Now I think maybe their husband died. It is astounding how one event can change your perception on everything. You might have thought spending your time putting yourself together before you leave the house was important and now it seems so time consuming and pointless.

It's these events in our lives that change our perception of what is around us. Maybe you have driven down this road a hundred times but never took the time to see the beauty of the landscape. Now you just want to take it all in and notice the small things that you took for granted.

This did happen to me. I had prejudices about certain people or things that I could not have been more wrong about. These are engrained in us as children from our parents or our environment. You will be surprised at how the view of the world changes when you are one of those people you would never think this would happen to. It is also very sad, because we were not able to change that view before. We were set in our beliefs. Really we only change those things when we need to. It would be nice to do it when we don't.

Over the last year I have met people, and seen those that have had a loss similar to my own. You look at them and perceive their lives were much like your own before the tragedy. However you would be surprised at how unique each situation is. So you can't assume they feel the same as you do. Everyone has their own path to "recovery". It is theirs to find and theirs to own. There were a couple of widows that I met that seemed to have it all together. They were able to laugh and seemed happy. I wanted to judge them and say, *"What is wrong with you?"* Some had lost their spouses before I had and I would think I had it together better than they did, only to realize that I was looking at them and comparing. If you learn one thing in all of this, do not judge or expect people to act or be like you. It is something we continue to learn . . . not to judge. I remember how I felt when others passed judgment upon me. I thought it was absurd.

What is important is that we are authentic with others and with ourselves. Being authentic is how we all should live, but it is hard. I think it is much easier to do once we are aware that others will judge us and we can brush that judgment off. Their judgments do not define us as human beings, they only show the person's skewed look at the world. It is not who we are, we know deep down our own truths. If you really want people to start talking authentically, give them the truth and they will share it. Being authentic is critical, it is about being in the conversation at that given moment and taking one conversation at a time.

One evening I had gone to the grocery store and was standing in line behind this woman. You could tell that she was physically crippled and she was telling me her story, about how she was in a car accident, and had barely enough money to pay for her groceries. I was feeling some empathy for this woman and thought to myself I am going to buy her groceries for her. It would not have been more than twenty dollars and I could afford that. Then at the very last moment she looked at my cart and made a comment that really proved to me that appearances are deceiving. She said, "And I don't have a husband like you to pay for my groceries." I looked back at her and I am sure I scowled at her just as I had done several times at my own mother when she said something I didn't like. I told her, "Well, sorry but my husband died. So I am paying for these groceries." I only hope that she thinks about making judgments and putting anyone else into a category. Needless to say, I didn't pay for her groceries and was mad the rest of the night about her comment.

Don't waste your time worrying about being judged or judging others by their appearances. Conserve your energy for the more important things that lie ahead of you. You will be judged and it hurts sometimes. Be the better person and leave all the judging up to Judy.

Use Your Crazy Courage

1. Your appearance can deceive others.
2. Your opinion about others will change.
3. You may see people differently than before.
4. People may say something to you based on their own perception. It may make you angry, so just walk away.
5. Keep in mind that everyone has their own grieving process.

People want to see you sad

It's not a bad thing. I believe that it gives people hope when they see you walking down the aisle of the funeral or at other events where you might show your sadness. It may help them to know that there is a man that was loved by a woman.

You may have sat there wondering why people expect you to be sad. Maybe there was a day when you didn't want to feel sad. You were so tired of crying that you refused to do so. When you don't cry and they expect you to they think something is really wrong with you. Well there is something "wrong" with you; you just lost the person that you had dreams with, who you planned on spending the rest of your life with. But you didn't get to and that is just not fair. So if you feel like saying, "I freaking don't feel like crying right now, I am not going to!" Remember, sometimes our thoughts are best to be kept our thoughts.

What I can tell you is that there were several memorial services that were held for my husband and some of them came several months after he died. I told myself that if I had to hear the bagpipes or hear his star number one more time I might run over and shove those bagpipes down someone's throat. At the same time, when I would look around me I would see the valor that my husband carried with him, the respect that honor gave him from all of these people standing around me now, and the story about his 32 years of life that inspired these people. Also, the gratitude everyone had for knowing such a wholesome person. The tears that fell down my cheeks would give these people inspiration to do what they have been longing to do when they had time. They receive hope that when they leave this world behind them, they will leave their mark behind for others to cherish.

I came to understand that people want to see you sad. It comforts them to see such emotion in a world that has seemed to have lost anything to believe in. So I embrace my tears and let them inspire those that need the inspiration.

When I think about it, I have gone to several funerals or seen mass tragedy. What did that do for me? It inspired me do what is important. Mass tragedy has united people across our own nation. It only makes sense that my tragedy would do that for others.

Use Your Crazy Courage

1. People want to see you sad, but that's okay. It will inspire them.
2. If you stop crying and feel people are judging you for not crying, ignore them.
3. Remember there are routines that make you cry over and over again no matter how many times you have been through them.
4. It is not a bad thing if people want to see you sad.
5. Sadness from tragedy can be very powerful. That power can be helpful.

Chapter Five
Live, Love, Laugh

You would be surprised how talking about things makes you feel better

There are times when you feel like telling everyone your story. How you met your husband and what was important to the both of you. I still enjoy telling stories about Mike. I tell his family stories that they didn't know about him. Sometimes I really get into it and do hand gestures or talk like Mike. Talking about Mike allows me to keep him alive through my memories; it gives my children a continued understanding of their father. This may sound strange to some of you, but I like to talk about the crash or even going through the court case. Unfortunately these are the only new stories I have of him.

Deciding to go to a counselor was a brilliant idea. I am paying someone to listen to me and not judge me for my own internal feelings. There are a lot of times that I speak about Mike and she listens to me. I do have friends and family that would love to talk about him, but sometimes I want it to be a one-sided conversation. Talking to the counselor allows me to be the only one in the room with information about Mike. Yes, I enjoy being selfish sometimes.

So here is my story written in far fewer words than the real story.

I am a 30-year-old widow with two small boys. How strange that feels to write. If someone would have told me that this was going to be my life, I wouldn't have believed them. My husband was a strong man that seemed undefeatable. I lost my husband on September 2, 2010. That morning was like any other morning. I was working at my home. My oldest was at school and my youngest at daycare. Then it quickly turned into the most heart wrenching day of my life.

I met my husband in 2005. He was just returning from his tour in Iraq and I was living with my sister in Seattle. My sister, Megan, had been telling me all week about how I need to meet this guy Mike, who worked in the lab with her. They were in the army together. She would say," I just know you will like him". I was hesitant because my son was very young at the time. I had to consider my child in a decision like this.

That Friday night after work my sister and I went out to a celebration for Mike. When I met him there was nothing really special. No fireworks that went off immediately, those came later. He was a very attractive man. He had a laugh that was contagious. He was also confident and poked fun at people. Who doesn't like someone with a sense of humor? We left that night separately, but I knew we would meet again.

The next day, Megan got his phone number and had me call him. The first time, I left a message for him. By the afternoon, Megan had asked if I had heard back from him. I said no. She insisted I call again. So I waited for a bit and dialed his number. This time Mike answered. I remember the words flowing out of my mouth so effortlessly. I said this is Samantha, Megan's sister. Then I went right to it and asked him if he would like to go out to dinner. He said yes immediately. So I broke into "You know I have a son right?" He proceeded to say, "Your sister told me". We set a date, which happened to be around Valentine's Day. Poor guy . . . no pressure or anything.

This is when our life started together. It was not any sort of fairy tale, but it was a life that was magical to us.

We spent that year dating and getting to know each other. Around Christmas he asked me to marry him. Well sort of. We were shopping for Christmas presents and he led me into a jewelry store. He asked me what ring I liked. The sales person looked at us and told Mike that she would look to see what our price range was. She came back and said he was approved for any ring in the store. His face turned pale and he started to sweat. He had a way of doing this when he was a little nervous. I knew that he was thinking, *I wonder what she will pick out.* The saleswoman was pointing at rings that were a little outrageous. My taste was a little simpler, which delighted Mike. I picked one out and we left the store engaged. It may seem strange, but he didn't need to get on one knee and profess his love to me. I already knew it.

A few months later we were married in Las Vegas. Only three people attended our wedding. My sister Megan, Mike's Sister Julie, and Julie's husband Jon. This was nothing spectacular in the world's eyes. I mean his suit zipped up in back, which still makes me laugh to this day. To Mike and I, it's all we needed. I remember afterwards, Julie asked me if Mike was crying when we said our vows. I looked at her and said yes with a big smile. I smiled, because it was those little things that made me love him and know he loved me. Wasn't I supposed to be the one crying on our wedding day?

There's a very important person that I haven't mentioned so far. That is our eldest son, Quincy. At first Quincy was beside himself with grief. Anytime Mike and I would be near each other, he would say "my mom". This later became a joke between Mike and Quincy. Mike fell in love with that boy the first time he saw him. Quincy warmed up to Mike and fell in love with this man the way I had . . . quickly. I remember watching Mike and Quincy play together; seeing their eyes connect and the love they had between each other. Perfect strangers in the beginning and then unable to separate from each other.

Over the years they played games together, had Nerf wars, played catch in the back yard, where Quincy experienced his first bloody nose. He didn't catch the ball and Mike came tearing into the house needing a bag of frozen peas, worried that he might have ruined the chances of Quincy wanting to play catch again. But they were out there as soon as the blood was wiped away throwing the ball some more. Quincy trusted Mike and that is why he looked up to him. Quincy's favorite times were when they would play "April fools" jokes on Mom. If you ask him, Quincy can give you every detail of every joke they played. These are the small things that only children seem to appreciate at times.

Mike and I added to our family a year after we were married. The first month we started to try, I was pregnant. The birth was not so easy. Rhyan was born by emergency C-section. I remember those horrifying days in the hospital. I was rushed away into surgery not completely understanding what was happening. When Rhyan was pulled out, he wasn't breathing. It took three minutes for Rhyan to breathe and begin his life as a newborn. Mike told me later that when he entered the room he saw his son lying on the table, blue with 3 doctors over him, breathing for the small fragile child that just entered this world. I remember Mike peering into my eyes over me asking if I was okay and telling me he needed to go to the lab to make sure everything was being done right. He worked as a medical lab tech in the lab that was testing Rhyan for any defects from the traumatic birth. I knew Mike and he needed to protect his family. Rhyan has grown to be perfectly healthy.

When I told the story, Mike used to always break the tension by sharing that when he was standing above me he saw a pickle sitting on my shoulder. He could not figure out how it got there. Well, I had eaten a cheeseburger for lunch and had thrown up with all the stress of the situation. Leave it to him to find some sort of humor out of a situation that had no humor at all. That was Mike.

After he served in the army, we made the decision to move to Arizona. This is where Mike began to serve as a United States Border Patrol Agent. He joined many brothers and sisters in green to protect the United States borders. He loved his job and those who did their job around him. He might have called in sick five times in the six years that I knew him. When he took time off it would be to take Quincy to watch the Phillies play in Arizona. The weekend before his death he took the weekend off. He spent time with his friends picking his fantasy football team. On Sunday he hung out with the boys while I had gotten my hair done. He gave me a hard time for it, because I told him we would have a family day. That evening we got dinner and made a picnic on the living room floor with the boys. It was special then, but has so much more meaning now to me. It was me and my boys, eating, talking and laughing. It was what family life was all about. Mike was always worried about not being there. He could not let anyone down. Mike was a person that stood by his word. He went to work early and stayed late. There were times when I would get frustrated with him for staying so late. I would ask, can't you put blinders on one day a week when you are driving north? Early for him, was leaving on time. I asked him that very question, only two weeks before he died.

We all have our own stories to tell. Some may be more glorious than others, but they are still our stories. I suggest talking about them to people that will listen. Telling your story will validate that the life you spent together was significant. This at times may feel less significant as you compare your time with your spouse to the time they had with their family growing up. You need to know that you are not less significant than anyone in your spouse's life. They chose to be with you and you chose them. You made an agreement of sorts to love and cherish each other every day of your lives until death. You both kept that promise and that is significant no matter how long that was.

I found that writing our life in a journal that I kept next to my bed helped me. I wanted to write them down for fear I would forget some details of the time we spent together. Honestly, you will likely never forget those details, because you will hear their voice interjecting as if you were there together telling the story.

There were also times when I would be sitting on an airplane next to a perfect stranger. I would mention Mike to them and tell them what happened. I did this not to get sympathy but to tell another person my story. So I encourage you, no matter how awkward it is to tell your story to people around you, tell it. Even if you find yourself in the grocery store crying next to the favorite food that your spouse used to love. That person standing next to you may be looking at you like you've lost your marbles. Talk to them, most of the time they will listen.

Use Your Crazy Courage

1. You need to tell your story, so tell it.
2. Talk to anyone you feel comfortable with, they will listen.
3. It is important to get a counselor.
4. Remember your story is significant and so are you.
5. Writing in a journal will get all of those thoughts out that you might not be able to share with others.
6. Your story may make others feel awkward, but you can keep talking unless they get up and leave.
7. Ask the person you're talking with if they mind you sharing graphic or intimate details of the situation.

Learn to laugh and be silly again

Being silly is the best part about being a parent. You can be silly with your kids and it is acceptable. I enjoy being silly and it took me awhile to find the silliness again after Mike passed away. My oldest son, my sister, and I watched this movie called "Air Bender". It was about people that had special power with wind, fire, earth and water. The next day my sister was kidding around with me, so we started an air bender fight. It is sort of funny, because my sister and I stood in my kitchen moving our arms around pretending to have special powers. My sister and I would then take turns falling backwards if we thought we got hit by one of the four powers. My kids would watch us and laugh. It was really good to hear them laugh. We would get frequent visitors that would check in on us, normally Mike's friends from work. So one day, though I am not sure how it got brought up, Quincy decided to go into detail about his mom and Aunt Megan's air bending fights. My sister and I looked at each other and broke into laughter. It is a little embarrassing but really funny that two grown adult's play around like children.

On Christmas day I saw my youngest child taking the stockings that had presents in it from Santa and putting them on his feet. He was like, "look at these socks!" Then a fantastic idea came into my head. I grabbed another pair of stockings and put them on my own feet. I grabbed the Santa hat that I had and told my children to watch me. We had tile flooring throughout the house, so I had them stand in the living room and I ran a few feet through the kitchen then began sliding in the stockings the rest of the way across the kitchen. They were amazed that you could slide so far. We ended up having a competition to see who could go the fastest and farthest. My sisters decided to join us. We even took some lasting pictures in these stockings.

I can remember one day being in the car with my two boys. I was really frustrated with life, the day, and everything else in between. My fuse was very short and I was yelling at them for being disrespectful. My thoughts were all over the place and as I was yelling, I became tongue tied. What came out of my mouth was something that none of us could even understand. I looked over at Quincy and he looked at me. He began to smile and I did to. We then broke out into laughter.

There were times when I would see something and it looked silly to me, so I decided to take pictures of the silliness. During my trip to Ireland my sister and I would create different poses for each picture. We did this on our trip to New York City as well. A very memorable picture was taken the night before her wedding. We had her fiancé stick his head on the top of this headless peeing statue, while my sisters and I struck other curious poses. A saying that became part of my every day sayings is "Who has two thumbs (. . .) this girl." Inserting whatever I wanted to after the two thumbs part.

Being silly is fun. You get away from any pressure for a bit. You reach in and grab your inner child, yank them out and do what they want to do. There are several things that I have learned to be through play. I learn about my children through play and about my own self during this time. A lot of pressure goes away during those moments of play, though it does come back. But sometimes it's about the recharge so you can continue to have the strength to use your crazy courage.

Use Your Crazy Courage

1. Connect with your "inner child" and be silly.
2. It can be fun to learn through play.
3. Remember, you are not too old to be silly!

Laugh because you have known sadness

Nothing helps you get through the day like laughter. Laughing makes you feel good. I am not sure what the exact science is behind laughing, but it must release some hormone in your body that changes the mood you are in.

There were many times in the last year that laughing saved me from a mental breakdown. During the funeral, Julie would call the funeral director the crypt keeper. This may sound a little bizarre to you, but for me she made me laugh through all the tears that were running down my face. I laughed a lot when people would say something that would piss me off. This was especially when they said the "wrong" things.

Something I heard more than once was that Mike was in a better place. That was the "wrong" thing to say to me when I was grieving. The only right place for him was here with me and his children.

I would think to myself that I probably would have said that to someone if I was in their shoes not even knowing the impact I would have had on the person. So for me it was funny. I was tired of being angry sometimes and just wanted to laugh. Then there are the times when I told stories about Mike and laughed. Laughter was another form of healing for me.

The day after I had first seen Mike in the casket we had a viewing. This would allow anyone that wanted their own time with Mike to do so. His father would go and sit with him all day. I waited until near the end of the day to go back. My mother, sister, a family friend, and I were leaving the house to go to the funeral home. As I was walking out my front door Mike's high school friends pulled up. I waited for them to pile out of the vehicle. It reminded me of a clown getting out of his mini car. Most of his friends were of a larger stature. As they walked up the sidewalk I caught their gaze. There was an uncomfortable silence with staring as we met each other. I told them that I was heading to the viewing and asked if they wanted to go. They looked at each other not expecting to get such an intense request the minute they got here. I encouraged them and said it might be good for them to have some time before the funeral tomorrow when there would be a lot of people around. Chad, Mike's best friend since they were little boys, seemed to take control and asked them the same question all over again. They agreed to come.

They followed our car that was driven by a BP agent to the funeral home. As we got near I told the driver to pull in. I looked over at the house and thought it didn't look that familiar to me. As we got out of the car I waited for his friends so I could walk in with them. My mother and family friend walked ahead. My mother tried to open the door, but something was blocking it. Just as she successfully pushed the door open, I realized we were at the wrong house and yelled at her not to go in. We all began to break out into laughter. We were all standing there on some stranger's porch, which I had mistaken for the funeral home. We gathered ourselves, got in our vehicles and headed down the road to the next house, which was the funeral home. We pulled up to the home and I think someone made some sort of remark asking if we were sure we were at the right place. We walked into the heavy front doors again. I was much more confident this time, than I had been the day before. I knew what I was going to see when I entered the room. I looked at Mike's friends and asked them if they were ready to head in. They said yes. The door opened to the room and we went through it. We walked down the path next to the pews. This time when I entered I saw the American flag that was draped over the bottom of Mike's casket. This was the very flag that was placed over his body after he was pronounced dead at the scene. On either side of him remained the honor guards. The honor guard had been standing next to his body for 5 days and nights now. They each took 8 hour shifts and stood completely still until we entered. When someone entered they moved away from the casket in synchronized movements.

This time I did not hit any invisible wall. I didn't begin to sob uncontrollably. I did hear the sobs of his friends. When I heard this I moved myself to the top of Mike's head and begin to stroke his hair. I looked up from Mike's face and see one of Mike's friends remain in the back of the room. He seemed very overwhelmed and unable to come near. Eventually he made his way down. He sobbed uncontrollably just as I had done the day before. This day I stayed calm and held in my emotions. I wanted them to feel comfort from me. I believe this would have been Mike's "job" in their friendship. I wanted to take on Mike's role in this whole situation. As his friend sobbed I placed my hand on his shoulder, then turned around and grabbed some tissues from the pew. I continued to rub his back. I remember questioning myself at that moment wondering what the hell I was doing. But I knew what I was doing. I was being a widow, a strong woman that was using her crazy courage in moments that many others might not be able to. I watched as each of his friends took their time with Mike, it seemed as though each of them shared their own words with him. Seeing this love Mike's friends had shared for him, made me honored to be his wife. After each of them had their time with Mike we walked out of the room. My mother and family friend went in to see Mike. After they came out, I went back into the room by myself. I needed to touch Mike's hair one more time. I rubbed my fingers through his hair and kissed his forehead. His lifeless body laid there in the casket with makeup on his face. The last time I saw makeup on him was in pictures from the first night I met him. He had passed out at a friend's house that very night I met him during his coming home party. Afterwards, our friends showed me the pictures of the eyeliner and lipstick they put on him.

I left the room that day with only one more day left to see his face. He would be cremated the very next day after the funeral. We drove down the road and I was dreading the next day. It was going to be a big day and would be emotionally draining. I didn't anticipate the amount of people that would attend the funeral. We went back to my home that afternoon and his friends joined my children in some sort of war game. Laughter filled the house as my children attacked each friend because the other one had coaxed them to do it.

It is important to laugh because you have known sadness. That day I led them to the wrong house, I could have stood there crying, but I chose to laugh. It broke so much of the tension that day. I mean these guys had just flown halfway across the country to see their friend in a casket. So you know what? If it is funny, laugh. Don't think that you have to be sad all of the time. It will lighten your mood a bit. I would think that at some point in time you are going to be so sick of crying that laughing is just what you need to do.

Use Your Crazy Courage

1. Remember to laugh because you're tired of crying.
2. It's okay to laugh if something is funny.
3. Remember that laughter can bring positive feelings.
4. When people say the "wrong" thing, laugh about it.

Better to have loved and lost that love, than not to have loved at all

This is so cliché, but I think it is really true. I am privileged to have experienced such a love. Our life together was a love story that I will always cherish and carry with me through my days. I am sure it wasn't that miraculous to others looking in, but it was to us. I am completely beholden for the time I was able to spend with Mike. I know that if I knew this is how our love story would end, I would choose it again. That is how I know that it was true love. This pain you feel inside is like nothing you have experienced before and you are not sure if you are going to make it through. Sometimes it was as if I was standing above my bed in an intensive care unit hooked to every life support machine available wondering if I was going to pull through. Seeing yourself in that state is unbearable at times, but you choose to breathe on your own. You choose to live instead of just breathe. I did not want to waste my breath, because Mike took his last one.

I believe there are people that go through life and do not experience love. Love is one of the most exhilarating and irritating emotions you have. You cannot force it and you can't stop it. There are soul mates. It's when you connect with someone on such a deep level that you truly feel as if your souls are bonded and will be for all of eternity. The movie "The Notebook" says it well. *There are people we settle for and then there are people we are meant for.* Ryan Gosling says something in a scene that is the inevitable truth about love. He says something along the lines of "we fight, you tell me when I am being an asshole, I tell you when you are being a pain in the ass, I am not afraid to hurt your feelings. Being together is going to be hard and we will have to work at it every day. But I want all of you." There is something to be said to wanting all of someone. There are good and bad things about everyone. You have to love them completely and take the bad with all of the good that they provide. It is what love is.

Our first date was close to Valentine's Day. What I know now about Mike that I didn't know then is that he put a ton of pressure on himself for the date to be perfect. He brought me flowers, which he would tell me later in marriage that he thought was a waste of money. He said they die too fast. Even though he thought flowers were a waste, he continued to buy them for me on special occasion, because I liked getting them. We left that night in his little Ford pickup. It was a stick shift and it was a little humorous watching Mike drive it through the streets of Seattle that were full of hills. Our nervous chatter on the drive there was pretty typical. With me asking a billion questions and him answering. He did mention that the restaurant we were going to was recommended by a few coworkers. We arrived and walked in the door. It was a very nice seafood restaurant in Seattle. We sat down and ordered our meals. Before our food arrived the waiter came to our table carrying a plastic bib. The waiter then placed the bib around my neck and set a mallet down as my only piece of silverware. The look on Mike's face was priceless. He was completely embarrassed. To him this was not the romantic dinner he had imagined. I began to laugh. He looked at me and laughed too, despite the fact that he was still horrified by the experience. He would tell several people the story about our romantic dinner wearing plastic bibs with mallets in our hands beating the shells off of our seafood, and then eating it with no utensils. He even told my younger sister that he thought I would never go on another date with him after that. How wrong he was about that. That was the night we began our story together.

There were times that I wanted to squeeze Mike's face so hard and kiss it at the same time. It always surprised me when I would get so angry at him and he would be able to wipe that anger away in a given moment. There were so many things that I loved about Mike. He was very genuine and he didn't care if he hurt my feelings. Well he did a little, but it was more about honesty. It was the way Mike grounded me. How could one person take all that you thought was chaotic in your life, wrap a rope around it and stake it into the ground? There were nights of intimate conversations we would have lying in bed, with his arms wrapped around me. He wasn't afraid of calling me out when I was being irrational. When I think about it our relationship is in those conversations that we had together. It was when I wasn't afraid of what he thought about me, that I told him about my deepest secrets. I knew that no matter what he knew he still loved me. We were able to remove the masks that so many of us wear and show our true selves with no risk. He told me he loved me every day, just as he vowed to do on our wedding day. I could watch him while he slept and think how handsome he was.

On the other hand he would irritate me when he would leave dirty clothes throughout the house. Or when he would have a short fuse when he was tired and be a grump. When we first met and we had an argument, he would walk away. I would chase him down until he told me what was wrong. Sometimes I would actually irritate him on purpose, just for the fun of it.

I can remember a few months before his death, we got into an argument. I can't remember what about but I can remember being mad and stomping off, walking up the stairs to our bedroom. He followed me, put my face in his hands and stood there until I told him what I was mad about. This was a lesson that I had taught him. He used it against me. It makes me laugh just thinking about the times we fought and there are only a couple of times I remember why. It seems very senseless now, but so appropriate.

I didn't get to see Mike on his death bed. I didn't even know he was going to die that night when he walked out the door. He didn't know either. I often wonder what he was thinking as he drew in his last breath. Maybe he was not able to think about anything because of his injuries. I ponder the choice, would I choose to have the chance to have a long death to say good bye or to die before I knew it. The answer is I would choose to say my final goodbyes even if it meant I would be in pain. I often think of what I would have said to Mike on his death bed. I would hold his hand and stroke my fingers through his hair. I would tell him that I loved him each day just as much as I did the day I fell in love with him. I would tell him that my life was better because of him, that he was the husband he worked so hard to be. He was the kind of father to both Quincy and Rhyan that would make anyone proud. He was a brother, a son, and a friend that everyone would want in their lives. He was my best friend and he let me be me. That I was giving him a piece of me to take with him and I will always carry a piece of him with me everywhere I go. That I will continue do my best to make him proud he chose me as his wife. And that I will love him until the end.

We have our own fleeting love stories to share. They will make you cry, laugh and bring back that tingling deep inside of you just when you thought you lost it.

Use Your Crazy Courage

1. Try to focus on the time you spent together and not the time you lost.
2. It's your love story and it was great.
3. You will cherish those memories of your spouse forever.
4. Talk to others about your love story.
5. Put together a memory box of your cherished moments together.

Learn to love again

Learning to love again is reclaiming what you lost. For some time I hated myself and my life without Mike. I began to teach myself to be in love again. I began to love my life and myself.

I took a trip to Ireland six months after Mike had died. I wanted to run away and get as far away as possible. I remember arriving in Ireland with my sister and feeling like I was able to hide from all of the reality the last months had brought. My sister and I made no plans on where we would go. We brought a map with us and would decide each day where our next destination would be. It was a good thing we brought the map, because the GPS the car rental place gave us was broken. We traveled North, West and then South. When we arrived in South Ireland, we had been around many parts of the country throughout the previous days and the countryside had wiped away a lot of my worry that was trapped inside of me.

One evening my sister and I walked up the street to a local pub. We thought it looked interesting so we went in. We were both captivated by the local music and some locals were teaching us some sort of Irish jig. I knew how silly I looked learning this dance, but didn't care. Returning to our seats I saw an older man that I believe earned every wrinkle on his face. When I approached he said in his Irish accent, "I enjoy watching you. I can tell you love life." I was surprised by his comment, because only days before I was not sure how to smile without forcing it. But he was right at that moment in the local pub, I did love life. This made me realize that loving life again filled my heart, leaving less space for the sorrow that I felt.

I spent the next few days driving through the last parts of Ireland we wanted to see. I thought about the man the night before trying to figure out what brought me to this place to find joy again. I believe it was the time I gave to myself with my own thoughts and to experience what I refer to as being "normal" again. This was my normal, not anyone else's. I gave myself a break from being consumed by the sorrow that had taken hold of me and was taking my life with it. I realize I didn't have to travel so far, but I did. My husband's death was very public and I felt trapped by people's judgments and what I was supposed to be. When I realized that I was allowing other people's judgments dictate how I was supposed to feel, it empowered me. Those judgments are for those people making them to carry. They were not mine.

I looked at my life in the last six years and thought it was amazing. Then I began to imagine how amazing my life will be when I love it again. I did not choose this life without Mike, it was chosen for me, but I could certainly do my best to make the most of it. I was now alone without my other half and I certainly did not want to feel defeated. There is too much pain with the feeling of defeat. I have met people that consumed themselves with their anger and you can just see the misery all over their face. I knew I was not going to live my life defeated. I may lose a few battles, but I was going to win this war.

You might need to start out small, maybe you should list all the things you love about your life on paper or even in your head, and then list all the things that you might not like about your life. Now find a way to change those things you don't like or eliminate them from your life. Trust me and trust yourself. You can do this. Make sure you concentrate on those things in your life you love and fill your days and nights with them. My most valuable gifts in my life are my children, family, and friends. I concentrated a lot of my effort on them, but still needed to concentrate some of my efforts on myself.

I did a lot of different things that I enjoyed doing by myself. I started painting my house and taking long hikes. I took several trips visiting my family and spent whole days watching movies with my children. I finished school and was proud of my accomplishment. I tried new things that would take up the time that I filled before with things I did not like.

I found out through experimenting that some of the things I loved doing before was because of Mike. It was the fact that he enjoyed them so much, that I did them and found joy for that reason. When I did them alone it was not something I enjoyed anymore.

Ask yourself: *what do I love?* If you cannot answer that question, find out the answer. Half of the fun is exploring and learning to love again.

Use Your Crazy Courage

1. Get to know yourself as an individual.
2. Stay determined to get through the grief. One foot in front of the other.
3. Realize you may change because of this tragedy.
4. Concentrate on what you love about your life.
5. Be willing to try new things.

Recreate yourself

For so long you were a duo. You no longer had your own personality and you identified yourself as a spouse. You need to know it is okay to recreate yourself. It is okay to be independent and be yourself. I am different now. I definitely have a place for Mike in my life; it's just not the same. I did not realize I was recreating myself until one day someone said it to me. I was showing them this new tattoo I had just gotten. That person said to me, so this is your way of recreating yourself. I looked at him, puzzled, but thought about the words that he just said. I thought about it for a moment and said, "I guess you're right. I am."

Looking back I realized that I slowly began to change those things that used to define me as Mike's wife. They were the things that complimented his personality. The things that make us our own unique individual changes when we get married. You alter yourself to become one person. When the other person is gone you no longer have the need for those personality traits. They are not important anymore. They might be for a while, because any other behavior would make you seem like a stranger to yourself.

Why wouldn't you recreate yourself? We are human and we are adapting to our new surroundings so we can survive.

In the beginning I was recreating based on instinct. It is funny, because certain characteristics that I know my life would lose because Mike was gone, I took on and recreated for myself to make them my own. I wiped away some of my own personality traits and took on a few of his. I read once that a woman who had lost her husband began to smoke when he died. She never smoked a day in her life, but her husband did when he was alive. It's not that smoking is something she would have missed, but it was something that was his that she took over for him.

Honestly I no longer had to be accountable to anyone but myself for the way I acted or treated others. I am happy I have high morals, but there are a few things that I tested out that just didn't work out for me. I wanted to have happiness all around me. At one point I thought about who I wanted to be. One day just doodling on a piece of paper I wrote . . .

Believe in me
Believe in who I will be
And who I was
Believe in who I am now.

I didn't even remember writing this message to myself until one day I opened that notebook and started to thumb through it. That message was very impactful. I needed to be able to believe in who I was going to be. I loved who I was and needed to trust myself to build myself as an individual that I would be proud of.

I evaluated all these things in my life and determined if it would make sense to change them or if they should be kept. I made these decisions . . . you know why? Because I can! It is important for you to create a person you can live with. There are also things that I did not change. There is part of me that needed to remain the same. Those traits that did remain make me Samantha Gallagher. What I changed was what made me the wife of

Agent Michael Gallagher. I do not think I could move on with my life, if I behaved as if I was still a unit with Mike. I wasn't anymore, I was my own individual. As crappy as that is, it was the truth and I had to live, because he was not able to.

Use Your Crazy Courage

1. You probably won't notice you are recreating yourself until you have already started to do just that.
2. It's okay to do it. You are coping with yourself as an individual.
3. At the end of big changes in your life, a new you is born with some of the same characteristics that you once possessed—just redefined.
4. You may find yourself wanting to change something about your physical appearance.

Chapter Six

THE DIFFERENCE BETWEEN CRAZY COURAGE AND GOING CRAZY

Wish it was me not him

There was a solid month where I wished I had died and not him. I was only hiding from the challenges that lay ahead. And there was a point when I felt he was a far better person for the world than me. It would have been easier for me to have died than for him. That is not what happened. He died not me, so I had to get myself back to reality.

I would stay in bed crying wanting my life to be over. I wanted all of this pain inside of me to disappear. The one certain way it could happen was for me to leave this world.

There was a big part of me that felt I could not live without him and needed to be with him. That is what I said to him on our wedding day. I would not leave his side. Now I was not next to him anymore, I thought I was letting Mike down in some way. I truly thought I could never be happy without him next to me. How could I be happy when he took most of my happiness with him?

At the same time I didn't want the pain to go away. I wanted to be stuck with it. I wanted to feel the miserable. I wanted to go with him. I wanted to talk to him and tell him about what had happened. I didn't want to face my life now without him.

One night I was talking to my sister-in-law and told her that I wish I had died and not him. She looked at me and said, "You can't think that way." Well I was, but by telling her my feelings and hearing her say that it brought me out of the self-pity.

You may wonder why hearing Julie tell me that I couldn't think like that anymore would make me feel better. If you met Julie and understood our relationship it may make more sense. She has taken a big sister role in our relationship. We are so similar that we continue to gain perspective about ourselves as human beings through one another. She gives me so much strength. We are able to have direct communication and forget about all the fluff that is so meaningless at times. She is capable of showing me how to hold my head high and endure what has been the biggest challenge of my life. The relationship we have is very important and so crucial to my healing.

It is important for you to get through the thought of wishing it were you that was dead. This will cause depression and you will really not want to live. But if you do not live than you will not be able to carry on what your spouse left to this world. You become one of those people that are wasting the air we breathe.

I needed to move on and face my unexpected unfamiliar life. I would not have been able to heal if I let this thought continue to consume me. It took time, but I got passed it. I had to continue to reassure myself. I was alive and need to live, because a very important person to me did not get to make the choice to live or die. At this moment I did get to make the choice to live or die without Mike. So I was going to take advantage of it and live.

Use Your Crazy Courage

1. You might wish it was you and not them. That's okay.
2. Don't dwell on the thought or it will consume you.
3. Find a way to get passed it. You are alive, so live! There are others that can't live.
4. Tell someone how you are feeling.

You do wish it was someone else

I don't know why someone would say they don't wish it was someone else, because I did. It always baffles me to hear someone say they wouldn't wish this pain on their worst enemy. Screw that thought. I would wish this pain and agony on anyone but myself. I wanted my husband and if someone else had to lose theirs so be it.

There was one day in particular that I remember having this intense feeling. I was at home, likely in the zombie state of being. The doorbell rang and someone came to get me to tell me that I had visitors at the door. I reluctantly walked to the door wondering who could be there. When I opened the door I saw three women. They were dressed very nicely and made me feel a little bit under dressed in my cut off jean shorts and tank top. They started speaking telling me they were wives of other agents that had worked with my husband. I could see the look of horror as this hit too close to home for them. They had all gotten together and brought me some gift cards. I was very grateful for those gift cards, because they bought a few groceries that I needed later. I know these women probably sat that day when Mike was killed and thanked God it wasn't their husband. During this whole conversation all that ran through my mind was that I wished I was them, walking up to one of their doorsteps and their husband was killed, not mine.

I cannot tell you the countless hours that I spent wishing it on someone else. But the reality is, it happened to me. I was the one that had to get through it. I never felt guilty and still don't for wishing all of this on someone else. I just don't wish for it anymore, because it is not going to happen. It is okay to feel this way, because you are only being honest with your feelings.

I think it is natural to feel this way. I mean who in the world would wish the emotional devastation on themselves?

Use Your Crazy Courage

1. You might wish it was someone else who lost their spouse. Having this thought is normal.
2. Remember to be honest with your feelings.
3. This tragedy may change your perspective.

You will have an episode or several

You're bound to lose your control and throw something in someone's face. I am not sure you can prepare yourself for those moments when you will lose control and have what I like to call "episodes". This is when your buttons have been pushed so many times, that you no longer have the self-control to allow people not to feel what you are feeling at that given moment. As small children our parents taught us what was appropriate to do or even the way to act when we are in the public eye. When people do not follow the so called rules of public behavior, they will likely be scornful. Not likely to say anything; just give you those nonverbal cues that we have seen for many years from our own parents or adults that mentored us throughout our lives. Nonverbal cues are engrained in us and our internal reaction to them was put in place from the first time we saw it.

There are two episodes that I would like to tell you about. They are very different from each other, but I still consider them in the category of losing all control over yourself.

There was a day when I went to the grocery store and really needed groceries. I went with seven gift cards that were graciously given to me by friends. So I had filled the grocery cart and was proceeding through to go stand in the checkout line. I always scope out the lines in the grocery store and watch the checkout person for a few moments to see if that is the line I want to enter. So I decided to go with the nice looking older lady. I wasn't in the mood to deal with any young person with an attitude and certainly one that didn't smile at you. She started swiping my items and I stood there in silence. She smiled at me and asked how my day was. I smiled back and said not bad so far. This was far from the truth, but I really didn't want to get into a long discussion. As she finished swiping the last item, I began to pull out 7 gift cards. I hadn't even taken them out of their little card holders. I glanced behind me and noticed there were a few people in line behind me staring. They were probably wondering how long it was going to take for me to swipe all those cards. I was at about the fifth card and looked up at the cashier. She smiled at me and started to giggle. I looked at her and began to get really angry, wondering why in the world was she laughing at me? I am only paying for groceries. Then she began to speak, "Did you just get married or something?" she laughed. I gave her a look of no remorse and said in an almost evil voice,

"No, my husband died." The look on her face was distorted. I could tell she was shocked at my response and really had nothing to say back to me. She looked around her to see if anyone had heard my words and was completely embarrassed. After swiping all my cards, I told her to have a nice day and walked with my cart out the sliding doors. As I walked to my car, I felt completely satisfied that I had taught that lady a lesson. When I think about it now, I feel horrified that I had felt pleasure in making someone else feel "bad".

I had several uncontrolled crying episodes. I would get to a point and wonder how my body could make so many tears at one time. There were two times that I wasn't sure if I was going to ever be able to pull myself together again. One was the day of the funeral. I remember waking up and being catatonic. I knew that I needed to be ready by a certain time so I got into the shower very early. I turned it on and sat on the ground of my shower letting the water pour all over me. I was in the fetal position just sitting on my bum. I was clutching my legs so tightly; I was cutting off the circulation to them. I cried and cried that morning in the shower. I wasn't sure how I was going to bring myself out of the shower to bury my husband that day. Then out of nowhere I heard my mother's voice calling me. It reminded me of when I was a little girl and I needed her coaxing to do something that I was adamant about not doing. But she knew that it was something I had to do or I would regret it. I stood up and stepped out of the shower. She handed me a towel and said nothing to me. I think she knew that she didn't need to; she just needed to take care of her little girl in that moment. Her gestures were better than any words that she could have said.

Your body will tell you when you need to lose control. I suggest staying away from sharp objects for a while, because there could be times when you throw the nearest object across the room. It is this feeling inside of you full of anxiety that is about ready to make you burst at the seams. You can't keep it in or you might explode like the man in *Big Trouble in Little China*. Let it out!

If there is a time in your life when you need to lose control, now is the time. At least you have a really good excuse for it. When you go through such a traumatic experience your body can only handle so much. I tried to keep my episodes in private. There were nights when I would sit in the corner of my room in the dark in the fetal position and cry. There were some great crying episodes that probably would have won a Golden Globe.

Use Your Crazy Courage

1. You will have at least one episode of "crazy" behavior, let it out!
2. Think about why you had the episode and what triggered it.
3. Learn from your episodes.
4. Exercise often to relieve some of your tension.
5. Cry when you need to.
6. Forgive yourself for losing control.

You are not crazy

I looked in the mirror many times, thinking I was going crazy. I wondered how anyone could live their life with all of these thoughts lingering. I am unable to focus on anything. I procrastinated and did not even do the things that I wanted to.

During the days before the funeral, I was not sure how to function. I didn't remember to eat and even didn't want to. When I fell asleep, if I slept at all, I would wake up each day reliving the truth like an Alzheimer's patient. I woke up crying most days. I woke up when the sun was rising and I would sit on the patio where Mike and I spent our time together in the evenings. I would say over and over, *I can't believe he is dead.* I would recite the words as not to forget them. I believed it couldn't be true and held onto the notion that he would walk through the door after work. This feeling may take time to leave you. You may not be ready to accept it. You may feel you are living in a false sense of reality. You are not going crazy.

I would meet people one day and see them again the next. I couldn't even remember meeting them. I constantly apologized for this, but frankly looking back I didn't need to.

When I would look in the mirror every day, I would see this person that I thought was crazy. I couldn't be normal and I didn't want to be. I could see the old me slipping away and didn't want to rescue her from the fire. I didn't care if she floated away, because I didn't know how to identify with her. I had not been through so much emotional trauma before and was unsure how to deal with it.

I went to a counselor. I needed someone to tell me that it was an acceptable reaction to the trauma that I had been through; that I was not slipping away and would not end up in a straight jacket with padded walls. Often, your brain is trying to catch up to your feelings. Some days it was like I was two years old again. You know how one minute a two year old might be throwing a fit on the ground and the next laughing. That is how my emotional rollercoaster felt.

Don't think you are crazy if you still talk to your spouse. I still talk to Mike and feel like he answers me. I usually do it when I am alone so I do not alarm anyone. They might think I have started to talk to myself. It gives me comfort to speak to him and to feel like he is still a part of my life. It's just a different part now, but I will never forget him.

A wise woman told me once that no one is normal, there isn't a normal. Now that makes so much sense to me.

Use Your Crazy Courage

1. You might think you have lost your mind, but the truth is, you are coping.
2. No one is "normal", there isn't a "normal".
3. Go to a counselor to confirm you aren't off your rocker.
4. You may forget all the details of a day while you are dealing with your loss. That's okay.

Don't just remember the good times

Remember both the good and bad. I think that sometimes people only think about the good times they shared. For me, I like to think not only about the good but the bad too. I think about the arguments we had. It makes me feel alive inside. Our lives were not only filled with happiness but also times of frustration. It makes it feel more real to me. Sometimes it feels like I would forget what it felt like when he was around. The last thing I want to do is lose those feelings. If I were to lose those feelings, he might be gone forever. Not even a memory would remain.

I don't want to idealize Mike; he was a person just like everybody else. He was his own unique person with pluses and minuses. We had a wonderful loving marriage, but we also fought just like every other couple. I believe if you idealize someone it will make it very difficult to be content again or even to move on. You are being self-defeating. What I mean is you are defeating any hope that you, yourself will ever live a life that is fulfilled without that loved one. We definitely will feel the loss and a part of us is missing, maybe forever or maybe we just might find it again.

As much as I loved the man, he frustrated me too. It would irritate me when he would leave his clothes scattered throughout the house, but it would make me laugh at the same time.

When we first got married my mother came to live with us for a bit. As much as I love my mother, there were a few conflicts that happen when a newly married couple has a mother living in the house with them. We got through it beautifully. It just caused some additional stress. The time Mike left for the Border Patrol Academy was particularly frustrating. We spoke on the phone every day, but we had a seven month old and a five year old to take care of. I worked full time and had to take care of moving to a new state for his job. I am thankful my mother was there to help me with that. What was awkward for us was when he finished the academy and he came back home after five months. I know it was only five months, but the kids and I had our routines in a new house, new state, and new culture. We all had to make some adjustments. He had to too. He had been gone living an almost single life. He only needed to take care of himself for those five months. This was something he had adjusted to. Then he had to come back and adjust to children and a wife again. That probably wasn't easy for him either.

There were also a few other things that we argued about, such as what was most important to spend our money on. What we did well together was compromise. We both gave our own argument to why certain things were important and why others were less important. We actually were able to make rational decisions even with our own natural biases. We didn't hold a grudge very long either. When we got mad at one another, it was typically for only what would be moments in our life together.

Use Your Crazy Courage

1. Once in a while think about those fights you had.
2. Think about those habits your spouse had that drove you crazy.
3. Remember both the good and the bad; it will keep your time together more "real".
4. Doing this combination may help you move on.

You may have a harder time letting go of habits

Don't rush yourself too much, some things just take time. There are many "bad" habits that we all have. It is always hard to stop these bad habits. I believe it is even truer when you go through such a traumatic experience.

For me, quitting smoking is especially difficult. Smoking is something that Mike and I shared together. I think I have the right intentions to quit I just have not been able to. When I quit smoking once it was like I am giving up another part of my life with Mike.

There were certain things that I had the habit of doing before Mike died. For instance, I would leave all of the clean laundry in piles waiting for him to fold it. I remember leaving it there for weeks, seeing it not folded made me wonder when he would get to it. Only he was not here any longer to do it. Another thing he did was scrub the pans that were difficult. He would see me at the sink trying to scrub the pan and say, "Just let me do it." After he died I would soak the pan hoping he would be there to take care of it for me.

On the other hand he had a few bad habits as well. He would leave a trail of clothes or dishes in every place that he was that day. When I no longer saw those trails, I would be angry that he was no longer here with me.

These habits add to the reality that a piece of your life is over and they are gone. I believe each day becomes easier to let go of those habits. Some you may keep and wonder when you will be okay with letting them go. I cannot tell you when or how you will do that, but I am sure it will come.

What I can say is prepare yourself for them, set goals for yourself, and if that timeframe doesn't work just readjust it like everything else in your life.

Use Your Crazy Courage

1. Keep your "bad" habits until you are ready.
2. Prepare yourself to let go of habits.
3. Take small steps to change habits if needed.

Being a widow calls to mind a certain connotation

You will go places that people will know who you are, they may not know anything else about you, but they will know you as a widow. They will know your story even if you didn't tell them.

There is something that I swear by and that is; get a big pair of sunglasses to shield your eyes. They make you feel a little less noticed.

Being a widow can connote that you have been through extreme emotional pain. If you tell someone you are a widow than they immediately change their perception of you. They immediately treat you with respect. It is a respect that comes from their compassion that they feel for your situation. You wonder, or maybe you know that they are treating you this way due to the sacrifice that your loved one has made. At times you feel like you belong to a society that is hush, hush. People might look at you and you may bring a sense of reality to them. You are proof that at any given moment they could lose someone. That is hard for others to imagine.

One of the most famous widows is Jacqueline Kennedy. When you think about a widow at a funeral it makes you think of her. She wore her black dress, pearl necklace and big sunglasses.

This is the type of connotation that I am talking about. It is uncomfortable, but take it in stride. One day you were just part of a community and the next you may be known by more people than you even know. It's another adjustment to make.

Depending on how public the death of your spouse is will weigh in on how the public will know you. My husband's death was public. We had newspapers taking pictures and our faces were in the newspaper the next day. It is really shocking and bizarre to see yourself. Luckily the news crews were respectful or someone did a good job of keeping them out. This allowed the funeral to be somewhat personal. I believe your spouse needs to be honored, but you should be able to make it personal.

I debated about the two reactions I could have. I could choose not to face the world so people could not see me in a vulnerable situation. My other option was to be proud to have been his wife and him, my husband. Sometimes you may not have your own identity with people. You will be known to them as widow of your spouse. I believe that when certain people see me they do not see Samantha Gallagher. They see me as widow of Michael Gallagher. It is hard to be an individual sometimes with that perception, but it's their perception, not yours. Be proud that you were their spouse and they chose you.

This could also turn into a good opportunity for you. People will listen to you. I am not sure if you have heard the song *If I die Young* by the band *Perry*. They reference a penny for my thoughts, but I will sell them for a dollar. They are worth so much after I am a goner. Even though I wasn't the one that died, I felt like people really wanted to hear what I had to say. It may not have been because my husband died, but at times it felt like it. I had that song played at his funeral. I had never heard it before until my cousin played it for me. After the funeral it seemed like it was on the radio all the time.

What I did was smile at people. When I would see their glances, but they seemed frightened to catch my glance. They would get a smile from me. People can't help but associate a widow with grief. Be strong for those that you will face and tell people how you feel. Think of Jacqueline Kennedy and remember how graceful she was and how she was able to survive in the public's eye after losing her husband who happened to be the President of the United States.

Use Your Crazy Courage

1. Buy a big pair of sunglasses or a hat.
2. Be proud, you were their spouse.
3. People will listen to you, take advantage of it.
4. Smile, even if you have to force it.
5. Cry when you need to cry.
6. Hold your head high.

Sex and dating

Sex seems like such a naughty word. Our parents were even uncomfortable discussing the subject with us as teenagers.

For some time sex will not even cross your mind. Well it didn't for me. One day I went to my yearly gynecologist appointment. I remember when my doctor asked me if I was sexually active. I said no. It actually made me a little angry. Why would she ask a widow that question? Well for starters it is part of her job. She must have seen the look I gave her. She said to me not to lose hope that it will happen again. We are all humans. I thought my doctor had lost her marbles that day when she told me that.

Until one day I realized that she was right. I began to think about sex again. My personal needs kicked in. For a bit I felt like a young teenage boy. I would see an attractive guy and would think of him sexually. When I did this I would feel my body heat up and I am sure the red embarrassment shot across it. Then I might be looking at a magazine and see a guy with a hot body. That would definitely make the hormones run.

Sometimes I would feel torn inside. You don't understand how you could think this way when your spouse is dead and for so long you believed that you would never feel that way. It is another internal controversy that you will need to work through.

To ease the sexual feelings, I decided it would be a good idea to take matters into my own hands, if you know what I mean. I invested in some nice toys. Only at first I would feel guilty about self-indulgence. It took me a few times to have my orgasm. All I could think about was Mike and missed what he gave me. I had thoughts that I was trying to replace something he gave me, but what I was doing was meeting my own personal needs. I also was unable of letting go of all conscience thoughts. Once I was able to let go of them again, I was able to have an orgasm. And oh boy, how I had forgotten how good that felt.

I would at times reflect on what my gynecologist said, we are all human. I felt as if I was having thoughts of cheating on my late husband, but he was dead. So how was that possible? I believe I was still not able to accept his death and that is why I was having these thoughts.

Dating is a big controversy when you are a widow. People will judge you for dating. My counselor's words of wisdom may help ease some of the judgment. She said using the word companion versus boyfriend or girlfriend may be an easier word to swallow for certain people. When

I first started developing feelings about dating someone, I had a lot of guilt. For me it was about respecting my husband. I was a different person when I met my husband. The situation was definitely different. I now brought two children that missed their father and I was a woman who missed her husband. My marriage and my new relationship are different. You still go through all those awkward things just as new relationships do. At times it may be difficult to work through those awkward moments because your last love life was taken away and not by your choice. You did not want to change it. I believe it is very important not to compare your new relationship with that of your late spouse. I respected my husband and still do. He is a part of my life, but just fits in differently now than he used to. I thought long and hard about being in a new relationship and if it was in any way disrespecting him. I determined it was not. My husband and I had many conversations about either of us dying. We more often discussed his death, because of the line of work he was in. We even talked about each of us moving on. There were only two things he ever told me about moving on and I respected those wishes of his. I never broke those promises I made to him and never will. I will always respect my husband.

Dating may be challenging. The challenge may come from outside opinion. I discussed this earlier, but I want to say it again . . . they are others opinions and are not yours. There may be a lot of guilt you carry for a little while for loving two people at one time. That is why it is important the person you are with understands and knows your situation. They need to be capable of being open and honest about their feelings. I believe they need to be capable of supporting us through our journey. It will not be an easy one.

We meet people in our lives and there are times when we are drawn to them. They allow us to feel the feelings deep inside of us. It's really hard to believe that you may be lucky enough to experience a love again, but you might. You may be able to look into someone's eyes and see yourself. You will see who you have become and appreciate that you did not give up. When they look back you may see the love they have for the person you are. And that is what I believe love is all about. Loving someone for who they are with all their pluses and minuses. We decide we will love completely and they will love us for who we are. Yes, it is possible.

Use Your Crazy Courage

1. Yes, you will once again gain back your sex drive.
2. Safe sex. Safe sex. Safe sex.
3. Meet your sexual needs if you have to yourself.
4. Date when you are ready.
5. Dating may feel awkward; make sure you are open and honest with your partner.
6. Do not punish yourself, because your spouse is no longer here. The forces of nature may surprise you.
7. You may be a different person now. You may find different things will attract you now when they might not have attracted you before.
8. You may be attracted to a person with the same values your spouse had.

Chapter Seven

WOE IS ME

There will always be a first

There are first birthdays, Thanksgiving, Christmas, New Years, your wedding anniversary and many more holidays that happen after your spouse dies. Even some things that you may not have thought of will affect you. It blindsides you and it is as if you were hit by a 250 pound lineman. You can't breathe and it's really difficult to get up from the fall. But you will scrape together the pieces of you that have fallen apart and put yourself back together.

For me it isn't always the day that gets to me, it's the days that lead up to it. There were times when I hid under the covers hoping that maybe the day would not come if I let it pass me by. I could have lived in my pajamas without a shower until someone complained about the way I smelled.

I can remember the first time I was blindsided. I was filling out a form at a doctor's office for one of my children. As I was answering all of the questions one came that I was not prepared for. There were four blank boxes and one needed to be checked. They said single, married, divorced, or widowed. I was not ready to answer that question so soon. My pen hovered over the boxes for several minutes and then with much anxiety I marked the widow box. I didn't realize that day I was going to get another reality check, but I did. After the doctor's visit I sat in my car and cried until I couldn't anymore. I drove away having one first under my belt, but not knowing how many more were ahead of me.

During the first few holidays I didn't really feel anything, I just felt numb. When our anniversary hit, I sat outside the whole night hoping to get some sort of sign from Mike. I cried for many hours wondering how I was going to survive another moment without him. There was a second when I felt like I could feel him next to me warming my body from the cold air. I wasn't prepared for the intense emotion that came with this event. I thought that I was "better". What I didn't know at the time is that certain events will make you feel more alone no matter how many people are standing next you to. And when you think you couldn't feel any worse . . . you can.

What I did was plan ahead for the holidays or events. So I did not get blindsided. It gives you a little bit of the control back to do what you want to do. If you want to have a big Christmas dinner then have one, but if you want to sit around all day in your pajamas and watch movies; do it. If you can plan ahead, know that the days before the holiday or event will be filled with anxiety waiting for that moment to happen. Maybe you need to plan for someone to watch your children so you can pamper yourself. It may give you the time to gain control of those emotions or maybe you need to let them all out with a kickboxing class. Do whatever it takes to be able to handle those events without a mental breakdown. If you have a mental breakdown, that's okay too.

The holiday that came by surprise to me was Easter. I remember running that day to the store to get the kids Easter baskets and had asked my babysitter to come watch the kids while I did it. When I returned from the store she sat with me putting the Easter baskets together. When she left I felt a sudden sadness that I did not feel before and it consumed me. There was a tradition that Mike and I did every year for the kids. We would make a trail of candy from the boys' rooms to their Easter baskets. This was an intimate moment that we shared together, laughing about the previous year's reaction from the boys. In the dark of the hallway I made the trails for the boys to find the next morning. At that moment I really felt alone and knew that the traditions we built would continue with only me, alone in the dark.

This holiday made me realize how important it was to me to keep some of those traditions alive. It also gave me the realization that I cannot let time pass me by without planning for the events that will bring the emotional rollercoaster back. I vowed that I would not make them stressful, but would plan ahead to provide myself with just a little comfort.

An event that I was not ready for was the first anniversary of his death. It brought back a lot of the feelings that I had when Mike was killed. It seemed a lot more complicated for me. I think it was due to the planning of it all. It wasn't a sudden surprise, like his death. I got through the day, the weeks before and after. What I learned is you need to do what is appropriate for you for this anniversary. It is and probably will be my biggest challenge for the years to come.

Use Your Crazy Courage

1. Plan for events and holidays in advance.
2. Keep those traditions alive that are important to you.
3. You may feel numb during events and holidays.
4. Stay in your pajamas if you want.
5. Talk about your spouse during holidays and events.

There will always be "should have, would have, could haves"

Everyone has should, would, and could haves. There are trips that you could have taken, places that you should have gone, and things that you would have done if you had more time. The whole reality of it all is you do not have any time. I wrote this letter to myself not too long after Mike died.

To you . . . the one who's eyes are full of tears,

If I would have known I would have appreciated every moment I had with Mike. I know I appreciated a lot of moments, but I would have appreciated those when we disagreed as well. I loved the way he used his hands to talk. The laugh he had that made everything seem so easy. The many opinions he had about the way things should go. The touch of his hand on my back when he approached me. When he would hug me from behind as I was cooking. The honesty he had when I cooked something he didn't like and the look that I would give him when he said it. The fact that all I had to do was ask and he would give me what I wanted or needed. The chills that I got through my body when we touched. The way he could make me so angry, yet feel the love between us at the same time. The way I knew where he had been in the house with the trail he left behind.

The look on his face when he was worried and how I was able to relieve it with a few words or a touch. When he called me a lion when I got up in the morning because the way my hair looked crazy from sleeping.

The way I could embarrass him when we went out and I would dance all over him. He would say "I can never go dancing again. I used to but one time I went to one of those dance clubs in college. I saw myself in the mirror and said I will never dance again". Except he would dance around the house, shaking his hips and doing the SCHWING (from Wayne's World) to make Quincy and I laugh.

All the firsts we had together . . . the way he trembled when he went bungee jumping together.

The pride he felt being a father and my husband.

The way his face looked when he slept or when we made love.

The way he bent over for me to scratch his back. The way he would say my footy hurty . . . can you rub them.

The way he would jump when I pinched his butt.

The smell of his sweat. The way he would hug me after he just got out of work and tell me to smell his armpits. Then laugh.

The standards he had for our family. The way he talked about our future.

The heartache I felt when he left for camp and the academy.

The way he would tell me that I need to stop worrying about things that were small.

The way he would click his pen when he was reading. How he would doodle in deep thought.

The way he would crouch down outside when he smoked a cigarette. When he smoked I thought he looked like James Dean.

The last weekend we shared as a family. When we had a picnic in the living room eating greasy food.

The hope he had for people that did wrong in their lives.

When he would think something was dumb and he would say fuck that.

The worry he had for being the best agent he could be. The calls at the academy saying he has to study more . . . he needed to get the best grade in the class.

The way he said I love you.

It is important for you to remember your husband or wife. I may not remember all of these little details in years from now, but I wrote them down.

I got this book for my kids; it is designed to contain information about their father. You answer many questions, even questions about his favorite foods, about their father throughout his life. It contains some really good information that your kids will likely ask throughout their lives.

There were many should, could, and would haves that I missed out on. My husband was taken far too early in life. I cannot change that. What I decided to do was do those things that were important to us and do them on my own. I will still do them, just not the way I pictured it would happen with Mike at my side.

Use Your Crazy Courage

1. Write a letter to yourself about the "haves".
2. Write down all the dreams you had together.
3. Consider the "should, would, could haves" that are still important.
4. Remember that we all have these, but they might feel overpowering now.
5. Try to find a way for you to validate your feelings.
6. Listen to close friends and family when they are trying to encourage you.
7. You will shed tears. Don't stop them, let them go.

You complete me

For some time I gave credit only to Mike for the accomplishments I had made when we were together. I realized though that the things you accomplish only get done if *you* do them. He was my companion and cheerleader of sorts. Surrounding myself with other people that would be supportive is what I needed. These supportive people do not replace what Mike offered me, they provide me with what I need in my life now.

There are many people that are willing to support you through this rough voyage you are embarking on. Evaluate those people you hold close to you to see if they are creating the positive environment you need to build your life.

I think a lot about my sisters. They are people I look up to and I continue to be impressed with their intelligence. They were capable of holding back their emotions when they needed to as I was dealing with such a painful experience in my life. They listen well, usually on the other end of the telephone. They do not judge me for handling things differently than the way they would handle them. They cheer me on when I need it and they believe in me. At times, I think they might know me better than I know myself. When I ask for guidance, they normally come back with questions until I give myself the answer. Their technique is very tricky and I know what they are doing. I appreciate it. They are what I would define as supportive people.

On the other hand there are people that are in our lives that are unsupportive. They might create an environment which makes you question your own beliefs or even your own actions. You could have taken the road that was scattered with halos and still it would not be the right path. They create a defeated environment for you and will not allow you to go to where you need to go. When you come across these people, learn how to identify them. Figure out what behaviors they have that create a negative environment for you. You need to eliminate these people from your life. If you are not able to eliminate them, keep them at a distance. They will only create more stress and negativity for you. You have enough to deal with, you do not need them.

If you do not have any supportive people in your life, you might try looking for a support group. When you meet with others that have gone through similar situations, it can help. Typically you can find someone around you that will be supportive. Do not be deceived by anyone that just agrees with you. That is not supportive either. Supporters also need to keep you grounded.

Use Your Crazy Courage

1. Remember that you have accomplished proud moments through all of this.
2. Find and keep supportive people in your life.
3. Eliminate or keep the non-supportive people at a distance.
4. Be thankful for your spouse's support of achieving your goals.

Instant happiness

Around month four I started desiring instant happiness. It made me feel better to shop, dance on bars, and plan trips. I wanted to celebrate my life. I wanted to try to grasp onto anything that would give me what I was missing, even if it was only for a brief moment.

I felt dead inside. I would have loved to get punched in the face to feel something. I needed to feel something because I was numb to the world around me. My new life was not exactly where I wanted to be at the time.

I am thankful for my children and my friends around me that kept me grounded. Without them I think that I might have lost control of who I wanted to be.

There is some good to instant happiness. It gives you a jolt that you need to survive, although taking it too far could be self-destructive. I tried things that I had never done before, things that I was scared to try. I decided one night to ride a mechanical bull. I tipped the guy a little extra and told him to make sure I stayed on it longer than my sister. That was a good laugh.

Instant happiness will get your adrenalin flowing but it only keeps you going so long. There is a time when you look around you and realize that none of these things will keep you loving your life.

You may go through this phase and trust me it can be lots of fun. Unfortunately it will only last for a short time. To really find happiness you need to look inside of you. We will never replace what was taken from us. All we can do is try to move forward because instant happiness is not going to fill that void forever.

Use Your Crazy Courage

1. Retail therapy can be good but only in moderation.
2. Dance on a bar if you feel the need, but keep your clothes on.
3. You are trying to feel something again. That is normal.
4. You will realize that the feeling only lasts a moment. That's when you wake up and find real happiness.

You will likely do something embarrassing while in the public eye

We all do things in public that are quite embarrassing. When you are in an emotional situation it can go from embarrassing to thinking that bad things happen to you for no apparent reason. I encourage you to know that it happens to all of us.

I went to a memorial service only a few months after Mike died. This was quite a large event and my seat was on the lower level. I was walking down the aisle towards my seat. I decided to wear heels that day and it might not have been the best choice. As I was walking over this mat the heel of my shoe got stuck. I stood there panicked like a deer in headlights. I was about ready to leave my shoe. Then a man jumped up and pulled my shoe out before I fell. I began to laugh. This caused a bit of a scene as well. Considering I was at a memorial service and others were mourning. I survived that moment, just like I have all other embarrassing moments in my life.

There were many times in front of others when I would cry and snot would be dripping from my nose. You know it's bad when you make a snot bubble.

These are just a couple of embarrassing things that happened to me, but it is okay. Really embarrassing moments are defined by each individual. When we go against what we believe to be socially acceptable is when we are embarrassed.

We are under more emotional stress, which can cause us to act differently than we normally do. Be patient with yourself and remember that so many other people are embarrassing themselves as well.

Use Your Crazy Courage

1. Don't think embarrassing things only happen to you.
2. Don't be afraid to embarrass yourself.
3. Remember everyone defines embarrassment differently.

You will be angry

This sucks, why did this happen to me? I had anger towards this situation; for lost time, for the fact that it was happening to me, and for many other reasons. I had a lot of anger. I would look out my window and be angry at people living their lives. How could they do that when I just lost what I knew as my life? I was angry simply because people were living.

The world looks like such a cruel place when you are so angry. You just want to make others hurt just as bad as you do.

I would get really angry at people telling me they were mad at their spouses. That just seemed so absurd to me. I did not even have a husband to be mad at.

I was mad at Mike for a while. I was mad that he was not capable of holding on, and not able to make it through the crash. I thought to myself that he must have given up, that maybe his family wasn't good enough to fight for. That quickly faded when I understood the severity of his injuries. His body was only able to withstand so much. Well, anyone's body is. It was the other person that was driving intoxicated that made Mike's decision that day, not his.

I was really angry and still am at the person that crashed into his vehicle. I did not understand how she was able to walk away with only minor injuries.

I think that if given the chance I may have gotten into a fight with someone just to yell.

Anger is a very hard thing to deal with. I think that exercising helped relieve just enough anger that I was able to control myself. Also an occasional pillow punching did the trick.

Anger is the biggest negative feeling that we get in all of this. We need to learn to deal with it appropriately. I think you should be angry. It is an emotion that comes with grief. We are forced into a situation that we did not ask for. Do not let it consume you. At the other end that will only create more misery. We have been through enough and need to focus on things that will benefit us through this whole situation.

Use Your Crazy Courage

1. Let yourself be angry.
2. Don't let your anger consume you.
3. Talk to others about your anger.
4. Get some sort of exercise to relieve some of the anger.
5. Punch your pillow or whatever else you can find. Just make sure it is soft.

Why me

Why me? This is the question of the hour. You might try racking your brain to think about everything you have ever done in life to deserve this cruel and unusual punishment. Sorry to tell you this, but you will never find the answer. Just know that bad things happen to good people. It really sucks, well more than sucks, but you already know that.

First you lose the person that you have shared all of your most intimate secrets with and then you have to face all the people that are a part of your life and appear human while doing it. Your brain then starts drifting through scenarios of all the horrible or not so horrible things you've done in life. You almost believe that you are to blame and you should have been a better person. Not one bit of that is true. I know Mike was an amazing person, but for a seemingly unknown reason, he was killed. I was not being punished; I simply had to realize that bad things happen to good people.

There were days or probably weeks that I threw pity parties for myself. I would sit around thinking *why me?* I can't handle another bad thing happening to me. I would lie in bed, wouldn't shower for days, and I was lucky if I brushed my hair. I didn't need to I was so engulfed in self-pity that my appearance was definitely going to show it. I needed to ask *why me?* I wanted to be certain that I somehow did not cause this tragedy to happen. I didn't want to be responsible.

There are so many times in life that we experience something new and we make excuses for not being able to deal with it, due to the fact that we have had nothing in our life that has prepared us for what lies ahead on our path. We become so self-defeated that we do not even try. I can tell you that there has been nothing in my life that would have prepared me for losing my husband. There have been times in my life that I felt sorry for myself and was unwilling to let go of the "woe is me". I made excuses and even tried to end my own life in my late teens. There are road blocks in our life that we need to overcome. It's up to you to decide whether or not you will allow yourself to wallow in your self-pity.

It would have been so much easier to not face my husband's death and given up, rather than do what I chose to do. Life is not easy and we learn from our experiences. We cannot sit around discussing why we cannot do something; we should be spending our time figuring out how we can get through it.

So one day, I built up the courage to go speak with the person investigating the crash. If I was going to be certain that I did not cause any of this then had to know the facts, right? So I took a shower, which was really rare at the time and got dressed. I remember the drive down to the station; I kept asking myself if I was ready for this. I knew I was, because knowing the facts was the only way I was going to stop questioning myself. I remember walking into the room and the investigator sat next to me. He had a stack of papers in his hand. These were all the papers that would tell me what I had been wondering. He pulled out the information about the crash, all of the mathematical calculations that were done.

He began by telling me the speeds the cars were going, the fact that the woman driving the other vehicle was presumably drinking. Well the blood work alone showed she was more than twice the legal limit, so I thought to myself; *I think I can take out the presumably.* The court proceedings hadn't happened at the time, so her side of the story was missing, but the evidence they had was pretty straight forward. Her vehicle hit his service vehicle near the rear tire and I know he had the right away. This caused his vehicle to roll violently. The investigator showed me the pictures of the vehicle. The rear axle was sitting detached many feet from the truck. You could also see the other damage caused to the truck from the roll over. I asked about the other vehicle and only the front bumper was damaged.

Mike died at the scene that day. He took his last breaths on the side of a road. This was very traumatic for me to hear. The response team did what they could, but he had multiple traumas, so there was nothing they could do to save him. After hearing this, it made me realize that I had caused nothing. It was the woman's choice to get behind the wheel after drinking that caused his death.

So I encourage you to have a pity party, ask *why me?* Just know that you need to get past it somehow. For me it was hearing the facts, for you it may be different. What is important is that you did nothing to cause this tragic event. How could you have, the facts are pointing elsewhere. We can't change the past, so focus on the future. When you have your pity party, if you can smell yourself and it makes your own nose turn up; that means you have done it long enough. So get up, take a shower, brush your hair and put some clean clothes on.

Use Your Crazy Courage

1. Bad things happen to good people.
2. You will never know why it happened to you.
3. Ask yourself *why me?* but don't dwell on it.

4. Throw a pity party for yourself, but you need to stop when you smell of it.
5. Stop feeling sorry for yourself.

Regret

Regret is a hard thing. We might have regret about our childhood or maybe we should have done something differently. There are times when we can eliminate regret by graduating college at an older age. Then there are times when we are not able to change the regret we have, because it is not possible. This regret comes with the loss of a spouse. Regret is sense of loss from an act or disappointment. We are in the middle of a loss or many losses right now. It only makes sense we will have regret. Likely you are not feeling one loss, but multiple losses. My husband was my friend, my lover, my companion, stability, and the many other roles he played.

You know that feeling gnawing at your insides, like a caged animal trying to escape? Yes, that is your regret. We regret what was to be our future. We do not get to experience this, because our spouse has died. How unfair is that? We know exactly how the rest of our lives together would have played out. Well, we have our own hypothetical best case scenario of what would have happened.

I regret not pushing the Border Patrol harder to let me see Mike after his car crash. In fact, I am still angry at them for thinking they knew what was best for me. I was angry at myself for not doing anything more than taking their word for it. I believe they told me they didn't think it was a good idea because of the injuries he sustained. I didn't care and still don't. It does not matter what he looked like. It is about me being with him when he was still him, not after he was embalmed. I feel like I never really got to say goodbye and have my own closure.

The other piece of regret I have is about not being there for Mike in his last moments. A while after his death I found a letter that I had forgotten I tucked away. It was a letter that Mike had written to me once, when he hurt my feelings. It said:

Dear Samantha,

You know you are the only woman in the world for me. I still feel awful that I hurt your feelings the way I did. Seeing you cry crushes me. My main goal in life is to be a good husband and father. You, Quincy and Rhyan are the most important thing in the world to me and I would die if I did anything to screw up our lives together. I really don't think I express how much you mean to me. These are just a few of the reasons why I love you so much:

1. You are beautiful
2. You are sexy
3. You are caring
4. You are sensitive
5. You support me
6. You are a fantastic mother
7. You brought me Quincy into my life
8. You brought me Rhyan into my life
9. You scratch my back
10. You poke my pimples.
11. You pluck my eyebrows
12. You are driven
13. You are successful
14. You are smart
15. You take care of me when I am sick
16. You're a great cook
17. You calm me when I'm frustrated
18. You give me so much even when I am a jerk
19. You are always there for me
20. You forgive me

You are the best thing that ever happened to me.
I love you will all my heart!
Mike

Number 18 on his list filled me with even more regret. At his biggest time of need in his short life, I was not there for him. I regret not being able to hold his hand, kiss him on the forehead and take care of him.

The funny thing is one of the biggest regrets I had was not being a bitch to my husband about coming home on time. I asked him only a few weeks earlier to leave on time. Mike could not leave work until he felt he did his job. The day his vehicle was hit he had stayed late to help out a couple of other officers. He started his drive back to the station an hour later than what he should have. The thing is, I am regretting a decision that Mike made. I know he made that decision many times. It was who he was and helped define his own unique character.

I continually regret the fact that we did not get to have the daughter that we planned on having. We were waiting to try until after my younger sister's wedding. I certainly didn't want to be pregnant during her wedding, because I felt it would not be as much fun. I pictured our little girl with dark hair and big brown eyes with her daddy's long eyelashes. She would definitely be blessed with dimples when she smiled because both her father and I have them. Mike and I would talk about her and say she would have all the boys in the house wrapped around her little finger. Mike would break in with his unforgettable laugh. How I would take her shopping and we could get our nails done together. The daughter we were supposed to have was taken away from us the day he took his last breath. Now, that was never going to happen. Maybe we should have just tried sooner. We did not know we were planning a future that was never going to happen because his life would end.

I would sit around analyzing many of my own actions over the months. Did I do everything right? What if I would have done something differently? I was only starting to take my own actions out of context. I was not looking at the big picture. What I needed to do was feel the disappointment and accept it. It's not easy and there was absolutely no way I was going to be able to change it.

I was so tormented by the fact that part of my life's journey didn't happen the way I had planned it. I regretted my children would not have their father at important parts of their journey to be a man.

We need to work through our regrets, because with this tragedy we will definitely have them. We need to step back and look at the big picture. It is important for our brain to work through the big and small questions. But this is our journey and only we are responsible for our own actions.

Use Your Crazy Courage

1. There will be regrets.
2. Question the regrets you have. Do you really know what would have happened if you did something differently?
3. Ask yourself; are you taking your actions out of context?
4. Regrets are usually based on best case scenarios.

Chapter Eight

HEALTHY LIVING

Don't push yourself if you are not ready

I didn't want to go back to work. I needed time for myself and for the boys. I made the decision to stay home with my children. I had always worked a full-time job and for the first time, I wasn't going to do that. I felt like I lost a little bit of my own identity when I did this, but it was worth it. Just like many other aspects of your life, you will change. Things that were so important to you seem unimportant now.

Some people may need to work. They might want to hold onto what they feel is important to them in defining themselves as an individual. We all make our own decisions that create an environment for us to cope with our loss.

Pushing yourself when you need to is important but not pushing yourself is as well. Each of us needs to find the place where we are in the middle. It is very hard to find that place, but you need to listen to yourself.

It took me seven months to watch our wedding video. I pulled it out and put it in the DVD player. As I turned it on I saw my brother-in-law walking me down the aisle. Mike was waiting at the end of the aisle for me with his sister by his side. I smiled at him and he smiled at me. I didn't know it at the time, but after the ceremony he told me the tuxedo he wore zipped up in the back. He had rented it from the chapel where we were married in Las Vegas. As I drew near him he took my arm, but in a very awkward position. I knew he was nervous so I readjusted it for him. As we said our vows we promised to be together until death do us part. There was an additional promise the chaplain asked of Mike and I. He said he wanted us to promise each other that we would say we loved each other every day and would not go to bed angry. I sat in my bed with tears running down my face and wondered if we did keep that promise. I answered myself out loud, because we did keep that promise. That day he took me as his wife and I took him as my husband. We did not know that his early death would happen. I thought to myself: *If I would have known that this would be where I was today, would I have gone through with it?* The answer was easy; I would have done it a million times over. The short time we were together created a lifetime of love for us.

In the month of May, I had six memorial services to attend for my husband. Some of them were in different states so I had to book tickets to attend them all. There was one I was unable to attend, because it was the same day as another. At the end of the month I had one more to attend. I decided not to go. I was exhausted from attending all of the others. Your body goes through a lot of emotions at each memorial service. You would think that after the first few you would be numb to your emotions; however I cried at each and every one of them. I was unable to control myself and it became more difficult as I went to each one. It was very hard not to go to the last memorial service. I felt like I was not paying my proper respect to my husband who was forced to give his life. However, I knew that if I went I would not be able to function for some time. I might have had a breakdown that would not be mended easily. I looked at my boys and knew they needed their mother to be capable of taking care of them.

There are other things that you want to do at the right time. Pushing yourself is good to heal, but it is not always appropriate.

All I can say is listening to your body is important. If you feel you are incapable of handling it, then don't do it.

Use Your Crazy Courage

1. Do not give into peer pressure.
2. Do not do it if your body is telling you "no".
3. Find ways to make time for yourself.
4. Everyone's grief and healing are different, do what you need to do.

Don't forget to get fresh air and exercise

Let me tell you working out some of your aggression and noticing that time does continue to go on with the rising and setting of the sun is important.

There were times when I became obsessed with working out. It made me feel so much better. Just days after Mike died I went on a hike up a mountain, like so many times before I had walked the trail. But today was different. I took the trail with a vengeance and ran down it like I was running away from a rabid dog. My sister, who was in far better shape than I was at the time, said to me that she stopped and watched me go down the mountain because she said she was in awe of how fast I was running.

If you need to climb to the top of a mountain and scream . . . do it.

I also began to train for a 5k run that was to benefit fallen officers. For anyone that knows me, I never enjoyed running any sort of distance. I was a sprinter. It was challenging to teach myself to run a pace. There were a few hiccups in the training, but I did it. I remember before starting the race I told Mike that this was for him. I know he would have been proud to know that I did it.

15 minutes of sunshine and a little exercise can do a lot for you. There is so much anger that needs to come out and what better way than exercise. You will feel so much better if you do it.

Exercising gives me time to think and cry. There was one day that I was running on the treadmill in the middle of the gym. I began to cry. I didn't stop running until I was done crying. Exercising helped clear my mind. It helped me gain more focus on my thoughts and stopped the reel from spinning in my brain. It really centered me.

Before Mike died we used to do this exercise video called Insanity. Our sons would do it with us. I couldn't even bare to do those videos. It would remind me too much of us. Until one day my son said to me remember when we used to do that exercise video together with dad. He explained to me how much he really enjoyed it. After that we got the videos out and started doing them again. It was time well spent together.

I challenge you to get up and get some!

Use Your Crazy Courage

1. Go outside and get some fresh air for 15 minutes every day.
2. Walk, run, or gallop, whatever type of exercise that works for you.
3. Exercise relieves some of the frustration.
4. Exercise will open your mind.
5. When you get to the top of your mountain, scream whatever comes to mind.
6. Exercise is a positive way to release your frustrations.

What to do with your life

What are you going to do with your life now begins with more questions than answers. People want to know what you are going to do. I had people ask me just weeks after Mike died if I was going to move back to where my family was. I didn't know how to answer them, because I didn't even know how I was going to get out of bed the next day. I have gotten that question so many more times since then. I usually throw in a joke and tell them I am not sure yet.

One day when I was meeting with my counselor I told her about this big issue I was trying to solve. I told her I had people asking me all these questions about my life and I didn't know what I was going to do. She told me; just tell them you have decided you are going to be lost for a while. That was a great piece of wisdom that she gave me. I wanted to be lost. With all of the other things that you had to decide, planning your life does not need to be one of them. You are not going to know this immediately. I was with my husband for six years and we planned our future almost every day of that six years. That is 2,190 days of planning. Putting that into perspective for me made me realize that all that planning has now changed. What I really needed to do was take some time to determine what was best for my family now. I am still unsure, but I do know how I want to live my life. I want to do things whole heartedly with such passion that my insides might explode. For me, there is a difference in what I want to do and how I want to live. I believe that once you know how you want to live; the rest will fall into place. There will be some decisions that need to be made, but when you decide how you want to live it will be easier.

I remember a few days before my sister left to return home after the month she stayed with me. We were sitting in silence on my patio soaking up the sun. I noticed her looking at me out of the corner of my eye. She said to me that everything will be okay, because I am a strong person. I began to cry. I didn't feel strong at all at this moment. I told her, I was not sure about that. I said I am just not sure how to pick up all the pieces and put them back together.

Our lives are defined through a series of moments where we either decide to live through or ignore. I read once that it is best to be in the moment, but in my circumstances I really didn't want to live in that moment. I wanted to run away and hope that when I returned my life would return the way I had remembered it being. This was definitely not going to happen. That was why I needed to have only one conversation at a time (another quote I read somewhere). With each conversation and moment I was building a new life. A life that I did not choose, but a path that I was forced to take, down a road that seemed dark and each turn was hidden behind a forest of unwanted trees.

Use Your Crazy Courage

1. It's okay to be lost for a while.
2. You don't have to know the answer to every question.
3. It is important to decide how you want to live your life.
4. You may change your mind about what to do with your life, it's okay
5. Don't ignore those moments that are happening right now.

Don't forget to take time to do those things that you have enjoyed doing

Getting your hair done, getting massages, pampering yourself is still important. You feel like a million people are pulling you in so many directions to get things done, but you need time to yourself to relax. Although relaxing is not what you tend to do when the room is quiet during the massage, you can still try. It's hard, because you feel like you should be miserable: that you should no longer have any comforts in life. You realize though that you need comfort.

When I was feeling really crummy I would get a massage or maybe get my nails done. During the massages I would tend to cry. I am sure the massage therapist would wonder if she was doing something wrong. Massages relieved a lot of tension that I had and gave me back a little bit of composure. There were times when I would start to talk and share stories about my husband. It seemed like being able to look in the mirror after a facial and see my skin glowing would brighten my spirits a little bit. I felt so ugly inside that looking at myself on the outside created a small illusion that I was okay.

You are not able to get a fast cure to ease any of the pain you have, but getting your hair done can immediately fix those dead ends you have. Pampering yourself is an immediate cure for your outside appearance and can give you the break you need for your well-being.

I am not sure if you have heard of retail therapy. Retail therapy can boost your mood, but you cannot overdo it or you will be paying the consequences for some time after spending the money. If you only have the money to buy something small for yourself like a new shirt, I encourage you to do it. Especially if that shirt makes you feel amazing. The next time you go out and wear that shirt it may give you the right attitude to face the world.

There will likely be some guilt after pampering yourself. It was worth it though. You need to create some positive energy for yourself to get through the days, weeks and months to come.

Use Your Crazy Courage

1. Spend some money conservatively to make yourself feel beautiful.
2. Relax even if it means locking yourself in a room.
3. Feeling beautiful may help boost your mood.

Life must go on

No matter how hard it is to continue on without Mike, life must go on. My kids had to return to school and at some point, I needed to go back to a "normal" routine.

There were times when I would look out my window and see my neighbors continue living their life. Sometimes it made me angry, but it shows you that time did not freeze.

When structure came back in my life it made everything feel a little less chaotic. It grounded me a little bit more. I started making to do lists for myself. It gave me somewhat of a schedule and a little more purpose to my days.

Getting back into a routine was a little forced for me. I had two small boys that had schedules. This provided me with the structure. I also went back to finish my degree. I had been going back to school when Mike was killed. He died two days before my final was due. Let's just say I didn't finish the final, but I passed the course.

You sit and wonder how life could go on. How will all those pieces of the puzzle fit together when there is one important piece missing? You may even not want life to rewind so you can live it again and again like the movie Groundhog Day. You want the ending to be your spouse living. We need to get up each day and move forward. Even though it might feel you continue to take steps backward and not forward. You will. It may only be one step forward, but it's a start. It was hard to go back to a routine, but it helped balance out my life.

Use Your Crazy Courage

1. Look out the window and see that life is moving on. Try to open your mind to it.
2. Structure is good for you when your life is out of control. It brings balance with it.
3. Make a routine that is at your own pace.

Forgive yourself

You need to forgive yourself for the things that you do that you might not have done under different circumstances. It is a lot easier to forgive others than it is to forgive yourself. If you can learn to do it and release a little of that anger and hurt, it will probably improve your mental health. Right now we need to do as much as we can for our mental health.

Forgiveness is very deceptive. One minute you think you have finally forgiven and the next minute the forgiveness is gone. What do we do when we forgive others? We try to understand the situation a little better. You need to understand the situation you are in comes with many uncontrollable feelings and emotions. We often play everything over and over in our heads. We are not capable of running away from our thoughts. They are in our heads and they are attached to our body. Who is better at beating ourselves up? No one is better than our own selves.

If we cannot forgive ourselves it may interfere with our lives. Right now you are trying to heal and be able to take steps forward. We want as little as possible to interfere with our life right now.

I want you to know you are who you are. At times we forgive people for being human. We should really look at it as; I can forgive myself, because this is who I am.

Trust me you're not going to forget the mistakes you made when you forgive yourself. You will just let go of the angry feelings you have towards yourself. We are focusing on loving ourselves, loving who we are and who we will be.

.

Use Your Crazy Courage

1. Forgive yourself.
2. Look at the person next to you and think if they were in my situation, would I forgive them? Most of the time you would. Use that philosophy on yourself.
3. If we do not forgive ourselves it may interfere with our lives.
4. People make mistakes.

Acceptance

How do you accept what you think isn't real? Tell yourself he is not coming back. Of all the different stages of grief this one took the longest for me. Everything that I had believed in and all that I knew about my life was taken in one swift moment. When you define the word acceptance it is agreeing to something, going through the process without attempting to deny it. That is a big issue when you are dealing with a loss like this. I refused to accept it. I did not want to go through the process, but at times you are forced to go through it.

There was astronomical guilt for me to accept what I believed to be unacceptable. I became afraid of forgetting Mike. I just felt guilty for trying to move on without him. I believe that part of my coping mechanism was to develop the saying—*What would Mike want me to do?* This did change what I needed to do for my boys and for myself.

During acceptance we need to think about the facts. Death is permanent and irreversible. Your loved one will never come back. We can remember the role the person played in our life story, but know that their story has now ended.

One of my friends would tell me, "Sam, stop, he is dead and not coming back." She told me this on several occasions. When I would try to deny what was really happening in my life I tried to avoid the process of accepting the death. I know she told me that a million times. One night we were sitting at a bar of all places. We were having our usual conversations and she said that statement to me one more time. For some reason, maybe it was that I was ready to do it, but I finally got it. I was ready to face my fears head on. I was ready to start the new beginning of my life without Mike.

Without acceptance we struggle through a false reality and will not begin to finish our story. It takes a lot of courage to face your fears and face them alone.

Use Your Crazy Courage

1. It may not feel real that your spouse is gone forever
2. Repeat to yourself what has really happened. Reinforcement is important.

3. If you want to, find out all the details of the death.
4. Ask for answers until you have no more questions.
5. You won't really move on until you accept what has happened.
6. Accept it when you are ready. Be patient, it may take a long time.
7. There may be several stages of acceptance.
8. Accepting will take away some of the burden, but will create a new sadness inside of you.

There is no timeframe

This is so challenging. People have their own ideas about what your grief timeframe should be and when you should do certain things. Only you will know when it's time. If you are ready you will know it. You begin to start asking the question . . . What if? Asking this is the beginning of knowing you're ready to do something. I love that people put timeframes on something that is an emotion or feeling. If we had the answer to this question we would be very rich individuals. Asking how long is just absurd. It's not like you are baking a cake and you know what temperature to set it at and put it in for 30 to 35 minutes. Timeframes are very complicated and each person is different. We are all unique individuals and if anyone wants to judge you for doing something too long or too soon, then let them judge. They certainly are not in your shoes and if they were it would probably be different than your own experience. There are many things to take into account for how you feel and what emotions you feel at any given moment. There are people that might spend six months being angry about it and others may take eight years. I have heard both. I think the other factors that play a role in the time frame are what your relationship was like and who you are as an individual. Every person is unique. If we were all the same it would be pretty boring. It will also depend on how your spouse died. There are other factors that will play a role as well.

You could even take two widows that are on the same exact day of losing their spouse and likely they will not be in the same period of grieving or be ready for certain things at the same time. If you ask most people they put a year on most things. I believe they think it lets you get through all the firsts. This may or may not be true. Once someone solves the mystery I hope they let me know.

Something I want to caution you about is allowing other people's guilt make you feel that it is not time for you to heal. They are only putting guilt on you. There is several kinds of guilt that might happen, try to learn about the different kinds so you can identify it when it happens.

About five months after Mike was killed I decided to go to a memorial service for another officer. I went that day to show support and hope it might provide me with some sort of movement in the right direction. Well it did not. It pushed me back in time and it uprooted a lot of emotions that I had four months earlier. I cannot say if it was the right timeframe or not, but it is something that I did. I don't regret it, I am just not sure if I should have done it.

I can tell you that it feels worse before it feels better. There were also certain months that I felt much worse than I did in others. This may not be the case for you, but it was for me. I had a really hard time and became stuck in month three, five, and eight. I don't know if it was what was happening around me or if it was something psychological. Month eight was filled with memorial services and this could have been the cause to my "almost" meltdown near the end of the month. Luckily my sister got married at the end of month eight. It created a little joy in what was a month filled with sorrow.

Once, when I was joking around about some of my recent behavior, someone said to me, "People understand if you are acting like that now, but if you are acting like that in six months I am not sure they will tolerate it." I remember thinking—Really? How the hell do you know that? If you could predict the future than maybe you should have told me Mike was going to die that day, so I could have eliminated all the anguish I have had to go through.

There are many questions, people put a timeframe on. The biggest question is—When will I feel better? I wish I could say you will right away, but you won't. Likely you will feel worse before you feel better. Then you will feel better and then worse again. It is a vicious cycle that I went through. Maybe you want to know when you take your ring off. I have heard people say they did it the very day it happened. Some people haven't taken their ring off ever. What I did was take our wedding rings to a jeweler, had them melt down the gold and designed a new ring that I wear on my right hand. I added his birthstone amongst the diamonds. Maybe you are wondering when you will get a good night sleep. That is a great question. I suggest leaving magazines or reading material next to your bed. When will you clean out his clothes? Not sure. It took me eight months to clean out our closet. I left his clothes on his side of the closet only taking out his shirts to wear to bed. When I couldn't bear to walk in the closet one more day, I took them all out and gave them to a friend to take care of for me. I did keep a few items and gave some to his parents and sisters. These are all things you will need to decide on your own. Do it when you are ready.

You might also be surprised about people's reactions to what you might be feeling or what you are deciding to do. Let go of any perception of what a timeframe should be for any type of event or circumstance. Do what is right for you. Use your crazy courage to get past all of those false beliefs. Live your life.

Use Your Crazy Courage

1. You will know when you are ready to move forward
2. Do not let others tell you it's not the right time
3. Dismiss any timeframe someone tells you. We are all unique and so is our grief
4. Question your choices and you will find the answers.
5. You may not be confident of the path you are choosing, but try it. If it ends up not being the right path, change directions.

EPILOGUE

What I hope for is that people realize all of the lessons that I have learned after my tragedy before a tragedy strikes them. What I can say is each of these lessons were hard to learn, but I pushed myself just enough to want to learn them. Sometimes I pushed myself too hard. I hope you might get some reassurance that you will see a light at the end of your tunnel with your own tragedy. I want you to look around . . . love, laugh, cry and live your life. Tragedy hit me and I learned a lot about myself. I realized how strong of a person I was. Every day was so beautiful and then it was as if I had forgotten how to breathe some days. I could have stayed in my bed forever hiding under my covers smelling any lingering scent of Mike that was left, but I didn't. I want you to know that I am only a small person in this big world. I will forever carry a piece of me around that aches for my husband and I sent a piece of me with him that day he died.

When I was young I believed I was going to be somebody some day. I am somebody; I am a widow that survived. I get to continue on with my life story, but my husband does not.

We need to remember that the part we played in our spouse's life is part of their story. For those of us left here, it is important we understand the role our spouse played in our lives and the place they have in our story.

I wish I had a cure for all things we must endure. I don't have that cure. What we can do as human beings is learn through what we read and experience. Our lives are filled with joys and heartache. Sometimes we focus too much on those heartaches and don't really see all the joy and happiness we have in our lives. We are breathing and living amongst each other. We look to others to lean on and some people are strong enough for us. Others may not be. We need to tell ourselves that those people who aren't strong are not going to bring us down today. If you have read this you are strong. You have been able to pull yourself together and face what lies ahead of you. You want to stop asking why me, you want to let go of the regret, you want to recreate yourself. You believe in who you can be and who you were.

When my time comes I want to be able to look back and say . . . I have lived my life. What I endured made me stronger. I want to be honored as my spouse was. To have a room full of people that care about me, making sure that everything went the way it should. I want to know that I was respected as a person. I want to have the word love repeated many times when anyone speaks of me. That is what I want my life to be about. I want to show the world what I am made of. That is crazy courage. I used my crazy courage to get through this unimaginable unfamiliar life I am living and I will keep using it.

You know mortality is a very uncomfortable subject for most people. They do not want to think about themselves dying or losing a loved one. Yet, it is something we need to talk about with each other. We don't know where our road is going to take us. We don't know if we are going to walk out the door and not come home that day. We are not in control of all things. We may believe we are, but we are not. This world is too big to control, but we can control the decisions we make.

When I was growing up, I was very angry at my father and mother. I believe my father began to crumble when he lost his own father. He decided to shut out the world for some time and that included me. He was trying to save himself some heartache if he lost someone close to him again. I felt he made some bad choices. He didn't want to feel, but all he was doing was filling himself with anger. My mother was very quiet and did not share her opinion about very much. She seemed to be sick most of the time when I was a child. I watched her crumbling within her marriage and with my father. It was a sad thing to see as a child and I told myself I was not going to make those same mistakes. I did not want to break like my parents did. I believe they worried too much about what they could not control and wanted to ignore the problems right in front of their faces. I believe they lost control of themselves, their emotions and their world around them had been broken for so long they did not know how to fix it. My parents finally divorced after Mike and I were married. This is strange but I was proud of them for divorcing. They were finally taking back control of themselves and their own lives. They are both strong individuals in their own way. They are also better people today for ending their relationship and focusing on healing from the long road they were on together. I do not think divorce is the right decision for everyone. We all know that people divorce for reasons that are beyond our understanding. Often we wonder why those people would get married in the first place. But I believe that was the right decision for my parents, even though they were together for almost 40 years. They found their own crazy courage in some way.

I did break when I was younger. I held in all those emotions and fears that I had. I used a mask to get through my days. I had been to a counselor for these issues that I was dealing with as a child. I realized that I was holding in that anger deep inside of me, unable to move on and be happy with who I had become.

I flew home one summer and was sitting next to my dad having a few beers, when it really hit me. I needed to forgive him. I looked at him and felt very young again, as if I had traveled back in time to the little girl that was angry. I told him that night that I forgave him for my childhood. That he taught me lessons and it made me who I was that day. I was content with who I was. And I used my courage to forgive my father.

I met Mike a few months after I returned from visiting my father. I am not sure I would have been able to open myself up to him, if I did not forgive my father that night. When I married Mike I was able to give him my whole heart, knowing there was a chance I could be hurt. I could have only given him half of it like so many relationships before had I not offered forgiveness to my father. When Mike was killed my heart shattered. I could have given up and shielded myself from pain as I watched my parents do for many years. I decided not to. I decided to believe in life and myself. I believed in love.

I am also not sure that I would have seen my parents cry at Mike's funeral and understand why they were shedding tears. There were very few times that I had seen my parents cry, but during this year they cried. They cried tears for their daughter and the life she was struggling with understanding. They didn't know what to do as I was trying to figure out how to comfort my own children.

My sisters cried, Mike's family cried and our friends cried. I believe they cried for themselves, but also for me and my boys.

People play so many different roles in your lives. They may wear a mask around you that comforts you, makes you laugh or let's you cry.

My little sister, whom I felt responsible for taking care of took care of me. I used to sing her the song *Build Me Up, Buttercup* when we were young and she had a bad day or even a week. I had a dance routine to go with it. She would be lying in my parent's bed and I would put the CD on.

One night when we were out at a fundraiser for my family they had karaoke. She had them put on that song and sang it to me. It made me cry and reminded me of those times watching her face turn from sullen to happy.

My sister Stacy was capable of being a rational person to turn to. She kept me from missing any of the small pieces of the puzzle that I was bound to lose.

Mike's sister, Julie moved in with me. She helped me with my children. She was there every day to listen to me, to cry with me and to support me. She gave up her own independence to give me and my children what we needed.

My friends and other family members gave me the advice that I needed to keep going. I got through this first year myself, but they all made it a little bit easier for me. That is what I needed.

Everyone has a bit of crazy courage in them. During this time you need to find it and sometimes it just comes out without ever knowing it is in you. Some of the most valued people in history have used this crazy courage to change the world. I am not asking you to change the world. I am asking you to pull out the crazy courage card and throw it down on the poker table of life. Because you just might feel like you won that poker game. That feeling is hard to replace and will give you back the control over yourself that was taken away the very minute your spouse died.

I challenge you to use that crazy courage to move on and face what scares you. It's a scary journey you are embarking on, but the adventures you have will be forever a part of your life story.

Michael V. Gallagher
July 5th, 1978-September 2, 2010

This was our last Christmas together.

LIST YOUR TOOLS TO FIND YOUR CRAZY COURAGE

1.   Lean on your friends and family for the support you need.
2.   Connect with your "inner child" and be silly.

LIST YOUR TOOLS TO FIND YOUR CRAZY COURAGE

SHARE YOUR STORY:

SHARE YOUR STORY:

NOTES...

NOTES...

CPSIA information can be obtained at www.ICGtesting.com
Printed in the USA
BVOW070834010512

289044BV00002B/10/P